# Warriors and Peacemakers

# Warriors and Peacemakers

## *How Third Parties Shape Violence*

Mark Cooney

NEW YORK UNIVERSITY PRESS
*New York and London*

NEW YORK UNIVERSITY PRESS
*New York and London*

Grateful acknowledgment is given to Richard B. Lee and Cambridge
University Press for permission to quote from The !Kung San: Men,
Women, and Work in a Foraging Society, 1979.

Library of Congress Cataloging-in-Publication Data
Cooney, Mark, 1955–
Warriors and peacemakers : how third parties shape violence /
Mark Cooney
p.     cm.
Includes bibliographical references and index.
ISBN 0-8147-1514-1 (clothbound : acid-free paper).
ISBN 0-8147-1567-2 (paperback : acid-free paper)
1. Violence. 2. Interpersonal conflict. 3. Homicide. 4. Third
parties (Law)    I. Title.
HM291.W315    1998
303.6—dc21                          97-45350
                                        CIP

New York University Press books are printed on acid-free paper,
and their binding materials are chosen for strength and durability.

Manufactured in the United States of America

10 9 8 7 6 5 4 3 2 1

*To my mother and father*

# Contents

# Preface

The social study of violence made enormous progress in the latter half of the twentieth century. We know vastly more about virtually all facets of violence than our predecessors did in, say, 1950. An impressive body of reliable information now exists on who kills whom, when and where killings take place, the nature of gang and tribal feuding, the interactional dynamics of violence, and the macrostructural predictors of rates of violence, as well as many other topics.

Even so, we know far less than we could, for there remain several underdeveloped lines of inquiry. One, perhaps surprisingly, is the role played by people other than the principal parties who have or are likely to have information about the conflict—third parties, such as relatives, friends, neighbors, workmates, strangers, or legal officials. A moment's reflection reveals that third parties must often exert a powerful influence on the course disputes take. They may be a force for violence or for peace, acting as warriors, peacemakers, or something in between.

The central intellectual issue is when third parties will wage war and when they will make peace. I argue in this book that the explanation is to be found in the social status and ties of third parties. Of critical importance is whether third parties are close to or distant from the principals, and whether they are above, below, or of the same status. Some combinations of third-party ties and status promote and intensify the violent handling of conflicts, transforming apparently minor grievances into long-standing and bitter feuds; others attract efforts to find a peaceful resolution of the disagreement, whether in the form of authoritative legal pronouncements by a judge or the amicable exhortations of a person caught between two friends quarreling.

These ideas draw heavily on the pioneering work of Donald Black. Black has formulated a body of extremely wide ranging theory that predicts and explains how people handle conflict—whether they will execute, boycott, or imprison; banish, negotiate, or sue; seek therapy, threaten, or demand payment—in every society, at all times. My own work, though considerably more narrowly focused, similarly incorporates data from anthropology, criminology, sociology, history, and other disciplines, as well as from two studies I conducted myself.

Although primarily designed to order some of the known facts of violence, the theoretical propositions I present in this book have practical applications, suggesting a strategy for reducing violence centered around two corps of third parties. In addition, I hope the propositions will encourage students of violence to explore third-party effects in greater detail. Indeed, should they do that, I will judge my efforts successful, even if the ideas prove to be misstated or, in the worst case, false.

For all the help, intellectual and otherwise, he has given me over the years, including comments on a draft of this book, I would like to thank Donald Black. Other colleagues and friends who have been especially supportive in a variety of ways during the gestation period of this book are M. P. Baumgartner, James Dowd, John Herrmann, Alan Horwitz, Calvin Morrill, Jeff Mullis, Barry Schwartz, Roberta Senechal de la Roche, and James Tucker. I have presented portions of this work at several conferences and received valuable feedback from many people, including Kit Carson, Russell Dobash, Richard Felson, Peter Grabosky, Richard Leo, Peter Manning, and Joachim Savelsberg. Leonora and Carl O'Sullivan read and responded to an early draft. Connie Kennedy helped with editing. Scott Phillips and Kerri Smith provided comments on the manuscript and help in preparing the references and tables. None of these individuals will agree with everything this book contains, but each has my gratitude for contributing to its evolution.

I wish to express my appreciation of the Department of Sociology at the University of Georgia for providing me with a hospitable environment in which to write this book. Earlier, I received support from the University of Virginia and the Center for Criminal Justice at Harvard Law School. To both institutions, I am grateful.

At a personal level, my greatest debt is to my friend, lover, and spouse, Mary Kelly. She and our two children, Nicolas Tendai and Zara, have provided me with more happiness and support than anybody deserves. Finally, in acknowledgment of all that they have done, and continue to do, for me and my circle of intimates, I dedicate this book to my parents.

# 1

## Introduction

It was a Saturday in September. They were having a function in a local park. Me and another guy, George, went along on bicycles. It didn't make sense to try and drive—there were too many cars. The bike George was on was stolen. As we were riding through the park, a guy came up to George and said that he was on his bike which had been stolen. George said it might look like his bike but it wasn't. The guy left.

We were in the park about an hour. When we were leaving, the guy who had come up to George before came up to him again. This time he had about five or six other guys with him. We didn't know them. The guy said that the bike was his. George said it wasn't. He said it was again and he then grabbed the bike by the handlebars. George told him to take his hands away. He said "I ain't taking my hands away, I'm taking the bike away." We started to argue.

The guy then told one of his friends to get a wrench out of the trunk of the car they was in. George asked him what that was for and then punched him in the face. A fight broke out. There were too many of them. One of them took the bike and put it in the trunk. The rest of them jumped in the car and left.

We went back to where we lived and suited up. We took a couple of sawed-off shotguns and some nine millimeter pistols. Then we went looking for them.

We saw them in the park leaning on the car eating spiced shrimp. Now there were just three of them. We drove by and parked our car in a back street. We got out and walked back towards them. When we got around, the guy who argued with George was the first one to stand up. I go over to him, and he says, "What's up." I say, "You know what time it is."

> Then he swung at me. We scuffled. Another guy joined in.
> The third guy reached into the car. George shot the guy he
> had argued with earlier. The other guy who was fighting ran.
> The third guy brought out a .45 pistol and was putting the
> clip in. He never got to shoot it because George shot at him
> but missed and he ran.
>
> The guy who got shot, Billy, died two days later.

These events occurred in a city in Virginia in the late 1980s. They were related to me by a young man, Tom,[1] who was serving time in prison for his involvement in the killing. Cases like this are quite common in America, where about seventy people are killed every day (MacKellar and Yanagishita, 1995: 1). But, then, few societies or large groups are free of lethal conflict. Violence, including lethal violence or homicide, is a fact of human existence.

Nevertheless, the incidence of violence per head of population (its rate) can vary sharply from one place to another. Take homicide, the form of violence we know most about. The United States has an annual homicide rate approaching 10 per 100,000 people (it fluctuates slightly from year to year)—about ten times higher than that of western European countries, such as England, Spain, France, Germany, and Ireland (MacKellar and Yanagishita, 1995: 3). In all modern societies for which we have information, the poor have more homicide than the rich, the unemployed more than the employed, men more than women, young people in their late teens and early twenties more than the elderly, and cultural minorities more than cultural majorities (see, e.g., Wolfgang, 1958; Strang, 1993; Silverman and Kennedy, 1993). The differences can be striking. In America, a twenty-year-old nonwhite male was, from 1970–1990, between thirty and eighty times more likely to be a victim of homicide than a sixty-five-year-old white woman (calculated from MacKellar and Yanagishita, 1995:

17–18). Among members of street gangs, homicide looms even larger, with mortality sometimes running at more than two hundred times the national average (Decker and Van Winkle, 1996).

Rates of homicide fluctuate even more widely across the structurally simple societies studied by anthropologists. The Mbuti Pygmies of Zaire, for example, have virtually no homicide at all. They lead a peaceful, cooperative existence hunting and gathering in the Ituri forest with little violent conflict of any type (Turnbull, 1965). Among the Gebusi of New Guinea, on the other hand, two out of every three men over the age of thirty-five have killed somebody (Knauft, 1985: 132).

Homicide rates may also differ dramatically in the same society over time. Medieval Iceland, for instance, was rife with feuds between rival families (Miller, 1990). Although its homicide rate is not known, it must surely have been high to generate that impressive but bloodthirsty body of literature known as the sagas. Modern Iceland, by contrast, is extremely peaceful, annually recording one of the lowest rates of homicide in the world (see, e.g., United Nations, 1996: 500).

What explains this variation? Why are some human settings remarkably peaceful and others strikingly violent? Why in one society are people virtually free from the risk of violence and in another exposed to it every day of their lives? The answer to these questions begins with a paradox: Violence is a type of morality.

## Violence as Morality

Violence, many people believe, is the antithesis of morality, the very embodiment of evil. But, as the sociologist Donald Black (1983) has pointed out, in reality violence is not usually committed for gain, monetary or sexual, or for the pleasure of hurting someone. It occurs, instead, as in Tom's case, in the course of arguments or altercations, fights or feuds. In the typical act of violence somebody seeks to manage or prosecute a conflict, to right a wrong. The wrong might be an insult, an unpaid debt, an act of sexual infidelity, or a physical assault. Whatever form it takes, it is a violation of standards of acceptable behavior that is punished by the violence (see also Levi, 1980; Felson, 1984; Katz, 1988: chap. 1).

To accept that most violence is an act of morality is not to imply that violence is morally right. Social science, as social science, cannot judge the rights and wrongs of people's actions. But it can say that, as an empirical matter, acts of violence are typically moralistic acts that originate in disputes over right and wrong.

It is easy to overlook this point. Newspapers, crime novels, films, magazines, and other organs of popular culture tend to concentrate not on cases like Tom's but on those in which people use violence to enrich or gratify themselves. Examples are homicides committed to facilitate a robbery or rape, and serial killings (see Dietz, 1983). These are not moralistic but predatory acts. The following case, again from Virginia, provides an illustration. The defendant, a twenty-one-year-old white man, describes what happened:

> One day four of us were hanging out, looking for something to do. Somebody suggested we rob the convenience store which was only about a five minute walk away. We talked about it and decided to go do it. I knew then I wanted to kill the store keeper but I didn't tell the others. I took a knife with me, everybody else was unarmed.
>
> When we went in the store keeper was alone, down at the back. Two of us grabbed him and the other two went to the cash register. The other guy with me held the store keeper and I stabbed him, many times. When he fell, we all just ran out.
>
> Why did I do it? I don't know. Just something to do, I guess. I had shot people before and enjoyed it but hadn't stabbed nobody. It was fun.

Most homicides are either predatory, like this, or moralistic. A small minority are neither. Infanticide, for instance, is typically a form of after-the-fact birth control committed by young women in desperate circumstances. And some manslaughters are negligent acts for which the killer is held legally responsible (e.g., killings by drunk drivers). But moralistic and predatory homicides are by far the most common types.

They are very different. Predatory violence is a kind of opportunistic behavior, unrelated to any prior conflict between the parties. Predatory violence falls within the same category of behavior as white-collar crime, piracy, and shoplifting; moralistic violence belongs with litigation, punishment, and mediation. Increasingly, scholars recognize that although the word "violence" is commonly used to refer to both types, they are, in fact, so different as to require separate theories (e.g., Block and Christakos, 1995).

We do not yet know how much violence is moralistic and how much predatory, but we do know that the great majority of homicides are moralistic. In the United States the percentage is between 60 and 80. In other modern societies, the percentage may well be even larger. Likewise, most homicides in simpler and earlier societies arose out of conflict, as the anthropological and historical evidence makes clear (see Appendix A). Unless otherwise stated, I therefore use the terms "violence" and "homicide" in the following pages to refer just to moralistic violence and homicide, regardless of the society being discussed.

## Third Parties

Violence is only one way people handle conflict. When does it occur? When will people like George and Billy resort to it rather than talking out their differences, ignoring their adversaries, bringing them to court, or dealing with the problem in some other peaceful way?

One possible answer lies in the nature of the conflict. People are likely to use violence when the stakes get higher, when the underlying issues are more serious. In fact, one of the odd features of violence is that it is not necessarily triggered by conflicts that other people would regard as especially serious. Even for a young man with little money, a stolen bicycle is hardly worth dying for. In that respect Tom's case is quite typical. Underlying many acts of violence are what to outsiders appear to be relatively trivial disagreements and insults (a point discussed at length in chapter 5).

Scholars therefore look to other places for answers to their questions about violence. One is the characteristics of the principal parties to conflict—the age, sex, race, educational level, employment status, and so forth of people like George and Billy. A second is the characteristics of the environment in which George and Billy find themselves. Criminologists have found, for example, that the percentage of one-parent families or the percentage of divorced males are good predictors of rates of homicide (see, e.g., Land, McCall, and Cohen, 1990).

Important as these foci are, there is another set of influences at work in many cases of violence that have received much less attention: other people who know or might know of the conflict. In Tom's case these people include not just Tom himself and the young men on the other side but the bystanders and even the police, whom nobody summoned. Had any of these groups acted differently, events could well have taken another course. By their actions and inactions alike these people shaped what happened that Saturday afternoon. Their technical name is "third parties" and this book is about the role they play in violence.

## Varieties of Third Parties

Third parties are all those who have knowledge of a conflict, actual or potential (see Black, 1993b: 126). People have potential knowledge when, although they do not know about this particular conflict, they often learn, by virtue of their status or position, of similar conflicts. Legal officials are the primary example. Third parties, therefore, can include family members, friends, neighbors, coworkers, bystanders, police officers, and judges.

Third parties shape conflict in different ways. Sometimes, they promote the use of violence by urging the parties to fight (perhaps calling them cowards if they do not), or by providing moral support or weaponry, or even by joining the fray themselves (see, e.g., Hepburn, 1973; Luckenbill, 1977; Felson and Steadman, 1983; Felson et al., 1984). In Tom's case, for instance, the groups of friends on both sides backed each other up, thereby enlarging the conflict. That very fact can increase violence. If it happens often enough, it can elevate the homicide rate significantly. Consider an example from Israel. In the 1950s and early 1960s, rates of homicide among Arabs were more than six times higher than those among Jews (Landau and Drapkin, 1968: 90). One reason is that Arabs, unlike Jews, were organized into large family units known in Arabic as "hamulas," the members of which have a duty to provide partisan support to one another in conflicts with other clans. Because of this, "a trivial altercation between two members of different Hamulas may develop into a prolonged and bitter conflict between the respective Hamulas leading to a vicious cycle of homicides and blood feuds" (Landau and Drapkin, 1968: 55). The same point could be made about urban gangs in the United States: by their willingness to lend mutual support, gang members escalate conflict, distribute violence more widely, and drive up the rate of homicide.

But third parties sometimes act as peacemakers instead of warriors. Indeed, the very same people who intensify conflict in one case can dampen it in another. Third-party peacemaking takes many forms, including encouraging the principals to run away, to talk instead of fight, to go to the police or some other group for help; championing a peaceful resolution of the conflict; distracting the parties from their grievances; or intervening to mediate or arbitrate the conflict. Informal peacemaking of this type is found in virtually every human group and is one of the principal mechanisms by which violence is curtailed or prevented.

Formal peacemaking is also important. Legal officials are the primary example in modern society of people charged with the duty of settling conflicts nonviolently. But the effect of legal officials on violence is not as straightforward as it might initially appear. Law undoubtedly provides a peaceful outlet for the passions aroused by certain disputes. But disputants sometimes reject the authority of the law and its officials and in the process develop a culture of defiance that creates more violence than there might otherwise be. Law and violence relate in complex ways.

Third parties, in short, can act as warriors, peacemakers, or something in between. The difficult part is to specify when they will be one rather than the other. Fortunately, there exists a body of theory that addresses that issue, allowing us to predict the behavior and effects of third parties.

## Black's Theoretical Paradigm

Third parties are an essential component in the innovative sociology of Donald Black. Black is probably best known for his theory of law (1976), but in fact he has developed a body of theoretical work that extends beyond law to cover the entire range of ways that people handle their conflicts (1993b). Indeed, Black has created a general theoretical paradigm—known variously as "structuralism," "behavioral sociology," or "pure sociology"— that, in principle, can be applied to explain any type of social behavior (see Black, 1995). This book applies Black's paradigm as well as many of his theoretical ideas on conflict management and third parties to the problem of interpersonal violence, and so it seems useful to describe both in some detail.

### Pure Sociology

Perhaps the central concept in Black's theoretical system or paradigm is the idea of a multidimensional social space. Every actor—person, organization, institution, society, and so on— has a location (or status) in each of five dimensions of social space. A wealthy individual, for example, has an elevated location in vertical space, a prisoner an inferior location in normative space. Every action has, in addition, a direction and a distance. The firing of an employee by a company has a downward direction in organizational space; a conversation between strangers from different countries takes place over considerable distance in horizontal and cultural space.

A key assumption of the paradigm is that social life is orderly. Particular types of behavior are associated with particular locations, directions, and distances, or more concretely, with particular social statuses and ties. The task of the theorist is to isolate the connections between behavior and social space, preferably in the form of testable propositions.

Take law, for example. One of Black's (1976: 21) propositions states: Downward law is greater than upward law. Among the wide array of facts this proposition predicts is that wealthy people in every society are more likely to take legal action, civil or criminal, and to be more successful in those actions, against poor people than the other way around. The proposition received strong confirmation from research conducted in the 1980s showing that in the United States, blacks (who are generally poorer than whites) accused of killing whites are considerably more likely to be sentenced to death than whites who kill blacks (Baldus et al., 1990).

The key to social behavior, then, lies in the statuses and ties of all the participants in an event—its "social structure." Whether a grievance will result in a lawsuit or who will win a lawsuit depends, then, on the social structure of the case, on whether the principals (the litigants) and third parties (attorneys, witnesses, judges, and jurors) are rich or poor (vertical dimension), intimates or strangers (horizontal dimension), organizations or individuals (organizational dimension), bohemian or conventional in lifestyle (cultural dimension), have a criminal record or not (normative dimension), and so forth. Together, these and other variables predict, in conjunction with their associated proposition (e.g., downward law is greater than upward law), the probability and outcome of a suit. Thus, some case structures are more likely to result in lawsuits than others. And if one city, state, or country has more litigation than another, it is because it has more conflicts with litigation structures.

There are several unusual features of this paradigm (Black, 1995; see also Horwitz, 1983; Cooney, 1986). First, it is not subjective. All variables are conceptualized at a purely sociological level. None requires the analyst to inquire into the state of someone's mind. Consequently, the paradigm is easily tested against the facts, a desirable feature in a scientific theory.

Second, the paradigm synthesizes many previous sociological approaches. Each dimension of social space represents a major strand of theory and research within sociology. The vertical dimension, for instance, is the province of Marxian theory as well as empirical investigations of social class, race, and other aspects of stratification. Similarly, the horizontal dimension incorporates much of Durkheim's work and network theory. Black's paradigm brings these and other traditions together within a single, powerful explanatory system.

Third, the paradigm is highly general. The propositions apply regardless of space or time, incorporating a large body of cross-cultural and historical materials. At a time when sociologists have largely retreated into the present (Elias, 1987), Black's paradigm is unusual in allowing, indeed inviting, theorists to develop ideas that apply to the entire range of human societies, to the Stone Age and electronic age alike.

## Third Parties and the Management of Conflict

People handle conflict in a myriad of ways. At various times, they fight, talk, run away, seek advice, ignore the problem, shame their adversary, spread gossip, go to a mediator or judge, seize a hostage, or take their own lives. Despite conflict-management behavior's apparent diversity, Black (1993a) argues that it reduces to five "elementary forms": (1) self-help (aggression), (2) avoidance (the curtailment or elimination of violence), (3) negotiation (joint decision making), (4) settlement (nonpartisan third-party intervention), and (5) toleration (inaction in circumstances where action is sometimes taken).

This scheme maps the universe of conflict management, placing both peace and violence in perspective. Peace, or nonviolence, embraces four separate categories and covers a wide spectrum of tactics ranging from benign toleration, on the one hand, to persistent, hostile litigation, on the other. Violence—which falls under self-help—is therefore just one of several types of conflict-management behavior. In some settings, violence is defined as a crime, but it remains at heart a moralistic response to wrongdoing. Importantly, Black (1993a; 1995: 855 n. 130) also specifies the principal conditions under which each of the five major forms is found at its most extreme. Criminal violence, for example, tends to occur among groups beyond the protection of the law (Black, 1983), an argument taken up and expanded in chapter 2.

Even more central to the present analysis is Black's work on third parties. Black, along with M. P. Baumgartner, began by distinguishing between settlement agents (e.g., mediators, judges) and partisans (e.g., allies, advocates) and developing a typology of each (Black and Baumgartner, 1983). In two later papers he takes matters further. "Taking Sides" (1993b: chap. 7) develops a theory of the conditions under which people provide partisan support to others and sketches several models of the effects of partisanship on conflict. This work provides the theoretical framework for chapter 4. "Making Enemies" (1993b: chap. 8) focuses, among other things, on the conditions under which third parties are more or less coercive, decisive, formalistic, and punitive toward the disputants. Chapters 2 and 3 are indebted to some of its ideas.

It might be noted that in addition to their settlement and partisanship roles discussed by Black, third parties can shape conflict more indirectly by affecting the moral culture of a setting. When rooted in the one place, when they have stable ties to the principals and to one another, third parties create an environment in which public opinion exerts a strong hold on people's actions. Everybody knows everybody else's business. Under these conditions, developing a reputation for honor or fearlessness can sometimes become extremely important to people. As many writers have come increasingly to emphasize, honor and violence are closely linked. Chapter 5 describes the principal components of the concept of honor and explores some of their origins in third-party characteristics.

## Violence

Black's work is increasingly influential (see, e.g., Horwitz, 1990). Several scholars have applied and extended it to a variety of conflict management topics. These include collective violence (Senechal de la Roche, 1996), international discord (Borg, 1992), avoidance and nonconfrontation in suburbia (Baumgartner, 1988), disputing among corporate executives (Morrill, 1995), cross-cultural patterns of domestic violence (Baumgartner, 1993), the treatment of mental illness (Horwitz, 1982), and the handling of grievances in nonhierarchical corporations (Tucker, 1998). Several of these studies will also feature in later pages.

One body of literature to which Black's paradigm has not been thoroughly applied, however, is aggression between individuals and small groups. This is interpersonal violence or violence for short. In seeking to build that bridge between Black's paradigm and ideas on third parties and the research on interpersonal violence, the following chapters do not, therefore, analyze violence at larger structural levels. Violence by or against the state, such as war, rebellion, execution, or genocide, for instance, falls outside the boundaries of the discussion (though there is a partial exception in chapter 2). So does collective violence or nonreciprocal violence by groups, such as rioting, vigilantism, terrorism, and lynching (Senechal de la Roche, 1996). Note, though, that since my conception of interpersonal violence allows for some violence between groups, the distinction between it and collective violence is clearly a fine one. But ultimately all forms of violent conflict, as Black (1993a) makes clear, belong to a single category. Hence, if there is some overlap at the borders, it should not matter, theoretically.

Most of the material discussed in this book relates to severe interpersonal violence, to homicide. Nonetheless, I have chosen to formulate the propositions more broadly, in terms of violence generally. Violence comes in varying degrees of severity: pushing and shoving lies at the minimal end of the spectrum; homicide accompanied by torture at the maximal. Hence, the conditions that produce homicide should, when present in less intense form, result in assault (see Black, 1993a). That may not always be true; there are settings that have a lot of lethal but virtually no nonlethal violence (Knauft, 1985). If they turn out to be common because lethal violence is qualitatively and not merely quantitatively different from nonlethal violence, my propositions will have to be recast solely in terms of homicide. Only time will tell, but in the absence of hard evidence, homicide does not seem to be a good candidate for a separate social scientific theory (as distinct from, say, a policy analysis). Whether somebody dies as a result of a conflict is often a matter of chance— the angle at which the bullet struck, the proximity of an ambulance, or the skill of the doctor treating a gun wound. Empirically, lethal and nonlethal violence shade into each other.

There is a pragmatic reason as well for focusing heavily on homicide in a book on violence: homicide is the best-reported and best-studied type of interpersonal violence. While studies of assault, especially outside the home, are scarce, the literature on lethal assault is both abundant and of high quality. A homicide is hard to conceal, so there is not a large "dark shadow" of unreported incidents. Consequently, the official (police, prosecutorial, and judicial) records are more complete than for any other type of crime. Thus, even though homicide is a comparatively rare form of violence in most societies, it provides the best window onto violence in general.

This book, then, uses materials on homicide as a vehicle for analyzing the impact of third parties on interpersonal violence. Since the focus is on third parties only, it does not present a comprehensive theory of violence. Rather, it advances a segment of a theory in the form of several propositions that explain violent conflict with the structure or shape of third-party involvement. Moreover, the propositions represent a kind of second-order theorizing in that they extend or elaborate ideas formulated by Black to explain self-help, partisanship, and settlement. Nonetheless, the propositions not only provide a series of hypotheses that can be tested empirically but, in addition, order a large body of findings in the existing scholarship on homicide.

## Four Foci

The social science literature on homicide, large and diverse though it is, can be divided into four main categories. Scholars have focused on homicide *patterns, rates, purposes*, and *conflicts*. The categories created by these foci can, and do, overlap in practice (see, e.g., Bernard, 1990). Nonetheless, they represent real differences in research and theory on lethal violence. Some of the categories devote more attention to third parties than do others, but none provides a comprehensive treatment of third-party effects. To that extent, research on third parties constitutes a significant hole in our understanding of violence.

### Patterns

The first category of scholarship seeks to describe patterns of homicide: who commits it, who are its victims, when and how it occurs, and what is the role of guns, drugs, and alcohol. Modern research of this type begins with Wolfgang's (1958) analysis of police and court documents relating to all homicide cases that came to the notice of the Philadelphia police in the years 1948–1952. Notable studies employing the same or a similar method have been conducted, for example, in Houston (Lundsgaarde, 1977), Miami (Wilbanks, 1984), Detroit (Goetting, 1995), St. Louis (Decker, 1993), for female homicide offenders in six U.S. cities (Mann, 1996), in Israel (Landau and Drapkin, 1968), New South Wales, Australia (Wallace, 1986), and Canada (Silverman and Kennedy, 1993).

The historical and cross-cultural literatures on violence provide more examples. Thus, Given (1977) has painted a vivid portrait of the social characteristics and actions of thirteenth-century English homicide killers and victims using court records of the period. Bohannan (1960a) and several other anthropologists carried out a Wolfgang-style analysis for seven African societies, using official records to describe the characteristics of the killers, victims, and killings.

Although this work has taught us a great deal about violence it has largely neglected the role of third parties, most probably because data are harder to obtain in that the involvement of third parties is rarely documented in detail in the police and court records on which it usually relies. Third parties, however, explain some of the best-documented patterns of criminal homicide. For example, scholars have discovered that no matter where one looks in the modern world—the United States, Israel, Canada, Australia—criminal homicide is strongly concentrated among socially disadvantaged people. But that is not true of earlier and structurally simpler societies, where homicide was often found at all levels of the social hierarchy. The reason, chapter 2 argues, is that there has been an important shift in the social status of third parties, especially legal officials, across the centuries.

## Rates

A second category of scholarship analyzes homicide in the aggregate, typically in terms of a rate per unit of population. Has homicide increased or decreased over the years, decades, or centuries? What explains the rise and fall of homicide rates in cities, provinces, or countries (see, e.g., Brearly, 1932)? Influential examples include Henry and Short's (1954) theoretical analysis on the relationship between the business cycle and homicide; Judith and Peter Blau's (1982) investigation of the role of income inequality in metropolitan homicide rates; Land et al.'s (1990) meta-analysis of economic and demographic predictors; Richard Block's (1977) and Carolyn Block's (1986) studies of Chicago homicide from the mid-1960s onwards; and Williams and Flewelling's (1988) work on the United States as a whole, 1980–1984.

On the historical side, Gurr (1981) has traced a long-term decline in homicide rates in Europe and North America. Bohannan's (1960a) book on homicide among certain African tribes also includes some information on homicide rates, an issue addressed by a number of other anthropologists as well, most comprehensively Knauft (1987).

Scholars analyzing homicide rates have also largely neglected third parties, again probably because of the absence of data. That is unfortunate because some of the effects documented by aggregate-level research appear to be third-party effects. Consider the well-documented finding that homicide increases with income inequality (e.g., Blau and Blau, 1982; Unnithan et al., 1994: chap. 7). As chapter 2 argues, inequality affects the third-party structure of conflicts. By widening the status gap between legal officials and low-status citizens, income inequality reduces the likelihood that disputants at the bottom of the status hierarchy will use the legal system to resolve their differences and increases the probability that they will resort to violence instead. Furthermore, the absence or unavailability of law has the effect, chapter 5 explains, of fostering an ethic of honor characterized by an aggressive sensitivity to insult.

## Purposes

A third category of homicide scholarship analyzes the express or implied purposes of people who kill. One tributary of this stream of thought is social-psychological and focuses on the subjectivity of actors involved in lethal encounters. Influential examples of this type of work include the ideas that coercion is a form of social influence by which one actor decides to impose harm or compliance on another (Tedeschi and Felson, 1994; see also Felson, 1978, 1982, 1984); that homicide typically evolves through a series of interactional stages in which protagonists seek to maintain honor in the face of insult or aggression (Luckenbill, 1977; see also Levi, 1980); and that killing is typically an act of "righteous slaughter" accompanied by humiliation and rage (Katz, 1988: chap. 1). A second tributary derives from Darwin, and explains patterns of homicide in terms of competition between men for access to and control over the sexuality of women (Daly and Wilson, 1988; see also, e.g., Wilson and Daly, 1993; see further Polk, 1994).

Unlike the previous two categories, work on the purposes of homicide has analyzed third parties. Particular attention has focused on the role audiences play in sustaining or defusing attacks on identity (Tedeschi and Felson, 1994). Scholars such as Luckenbill (1977) and Felson (1982; Felson and Steadman, 1983; Felson et al., 1984; Felson and Russo, 1988) have shown that the course of confrontations can be dramatically affected by the actions of third-party audiences. Third parties can provide the principals with face-saving alternatives to violence, but they can also, by their words, deeds, or mere presence, encourage the principal protagonists to be violent (see also Oliver, 1994). Valuable though this work is (and later chapters draw upon it at several points), it does not provide a systematic theory specifying when third parties will adopt one role rather than the other.

## Conflicts

The final category of scholarship is the most compatible with the Blackian theoretical paradigm because it treats homicide in the context of conflict. While conflict may be a theme of the previous categories, (especially the third), it is the central focus of the information provided on homicide by both branches of this fourth category. The first branch consists of field studies of gang violence in, for example, Chicago (Thrasher, 1927; Horowitz, 1983), Los Angeles (Klein, 1971; Moore et al., 1978), Milwaukee (Hagedorn, 1988), and St. Louis (Decker and Van Winkle, 1996). The second branch of conflict-related homicide scholarship uses biography to shed light on the social contexts of the low-income neighborhoods and social groups in which most violence today tends to be concentrated. Examples of this important new genre include accounts of life in a Los Angeles gang (Shakur, 1993), growing up in a tough part of New York (Canada, 1995), and the transmission of violence across the generations within an American family (Butterfield, 1995).

Historians, too, have not neglected lethal conflict. Stone's (1965) influential work on the Tudor and early Stuart English aristocracy includes some fascinating information on violence. Dueling has attracted the interest of several scholars, both with respect to its European (Kiernan, 1988; Kelly, 1995) and North American varieties (Wyatt-Brown, 1982; Williams, 1980). Less formal types of nineteenth-century American violence have been discussed by McGrath (1984) in his study of gunfighting in two western mining towns and by Ayers (1984) in his overview of southern crime and justice.

Anthropologists, similarly, have written extensively on violent conflict among, for instance, the Nuer of the Sudan (Evans-Pritchard, 1940), the Yanomamö of Venezuela-Brazil (Chagnon, 1977), the Tausug of the Philippines (Kiefer, 1972), and the Ju/'hoansi of Botswana (Lee, 1979, 1993), to name but a few. Many New Guinea ethnographers have presented important data and insights on violence (see, e.g., Koch, 1974; Hallpike, 1977; Knauft, 1985). Boehm (1984) and Black-Michaud (1975) have published informative specialized studies of feuding. And Pitt-Rivers (1966) has written insightfully and influentially on the role of honor in violence.

Scholarship that treats homicide as conflict does discuss the effect of third parties on, for example, gang violence, preindustrial feuding, and honor. For the most part, however, these discussions of third parties are unsystematic. Scattered through the conflict literature—especially cross-cultural work—are references, anecdotes, findings, examples, comments, and suggestions relating to a wide range of third-party behavior. Although these sources do not provide answers to all the major questions, they do constitute a substantial initial body of data.

## My Data

In organizing the literature on third parties, I also draw on two studies I conducted of homicide. The first is a series of interviews with sixty-three men and twelve women imprisoned for murder and manslaughter in Virginia during 1988. The interviews focused on, among other things, the background of each killing, its history and genesis. In addition, I interviewed, by telephone, whenever the prisoner agreed and I could make contact, a member of the prisoner's family, usually his or her mother. To corroborate the information obtained, I read, where available, the prisoner's Pre-sentence Investigation Report used by the court in passing sentence (Cooney, 1991).

Because seventy-five homicides is a relatively small sample, I use these interviews not for the purposes of making generalizations but to provide illustrative cases. Their purpose is to enrich and enliven the narrative, to bring home to the reader the social reality of homicide. Where there is a discrepancy between the prisoner's and the official version of the facts, I note it in the text. (For further details of the study, see Appendix B.)

My second study analyzed the social control or the typical response to homicide in ten relationships (e.g., husband-wife, male neighbors) across thirty preindustrial societies (Cooney, 1988). Of the three hundred possible relationships, information was available on ninety. In some of the relationships, third parties will avenge the killing; in others they will respond peacefully. Their behavior can thus throw light on the social conditions underlying third-party peace and violence for roughly the same initial offense. (Appendix C describes this study in more detail.) In discussing this study and the cross-cultural literature more generally, I will typically use the convention known as the "ethnographic present tense" to refer to these societies, even though most, perhaps all, no longer exist in the form described by anthropologists.

In summary, although violence is found virtually everywhere human beings congregate in any numbers, it varies enormously in frequency. Some settings generate virtually no violence at all—the occasional slap or push, perhaps, but no dangerous assaults or killings. Others produce enormous amounts—not just pushing and slapping but kicking, beating, biting, gouging, stabbing, and shooting are regular occurrences, everywhere in evidence.

To explain this variation, it is necessary to look more widely than the principals but more narrowly than the macroenvironment, at third parties. Third parties shape conflict in two senses: they affect the behavior of those involved, directly and indirectly, and they alter the structure of the conflict in social space.

Tom's case, for example, cannot be understood by focusing just on George and Billy. Any of the other men involved could equally well have been killed or carried out the killing. Moreover, the bystanders and police were unwilling or unable to stop the violence and hence they too are central to the events that took place that September Saturday.

Tom's case is not an exception. Third parties can be warriors or peacemakers, a force for violent retaliation or for one of several forms of peace. The next three chapters adopt Donald Black's theoretical strategy and some of his ideas to present several propositions that link variation in the shapes third parties bring to conflicts and their outcome. The propositions are theoretical, predicting and explaining a large body of empirical findings in modern and premodern societies alike. But they have other uses as well. They suggest several lines of empirical inquiry for the future as well a strategy for reducing violence, issues that are addressed in the final chapter. The chapters that follow, then, may be of interest to those concerned with violence from a variety of perspectives.

# 2

# The U-Curve of Violence 1

Chuck and I fought all the time. Like cats and dogs. He beat me. The only way I could get him off was to draw a knife on him.

This one morning I got up early and went to the methadone clinic. When Chuck got up, we went to the 7-11 [i.e., convenience store] and got coffee. He was sick. I had only $14 but I gave it to him for dope. We went on bicycles to try and score. We met some people we knew and Chuck shot up behind this old house. Chuck got into an argument then with some girls who were there. They turned on me. I threw a knife at one of them and ran. On the way home I stopped at a bootlegging house for a beer, to steady my nerves. Chuck came a few minutes later. He was completely off. I had never seen him like this—shouting, screaming, cussing, fussing.

I went home and told my kids to get their things together because we were going over to my mother's house for a while. As they were doing this, Chuck arrived home—still ragin' and pagin'. I was scared. I went into the kitchen and got a knife. I knew from experience that he wouldn't hit me if I had one. But this time he grabbed me and slammed me hard up against the wall. As I came off the third time, I hit him with the knife in the chest. He backed out the door and down the steps. I grabbed my kids and left. That was the last time I saw Chuck alive.

In the official version of the case, the narrator, Stephanie, and Chuck were arguing outside her house because he had not supported her in the earlier confrontation. Regardless of the exact details, Stephanie admits she killed Chuck in the course of a dispute.

Every homicide is a mixture of the unique and the typical. One of the typical features of this case is the disadvantaged background of Stephanie and Chuck. In all modern societies that we know about, violence, especially intense violence like homicide, is largely confined to people of low social status. Curiously, though, this was not so in earlier times where violent conflict was found at all levels of the social hierarchy, including the top.

Why is this? Why is violence today concentrated at the lower end of the status hierarchy? Why has elite violence virtually disappeared? The answer to these questions can be found in the social status of third parties. Third parties who are high above the principal parties in status—as legal officials today are with respect to low-status citizens—tend to be repressive and unpopular with disputants who reject their authority (Black, 1993b: chap. 8). And without third parties to help settle disputes, violence becomes more likely.

But violence also occurs when third parties are not above the status of the principals at all. Third parties who are no higher than the principals in status—as legal officials in early states were with respect to elites—are unlikely to have their services sought out by disputants (Black and Baumgartner, 1983: 113). It is between these extremes that the probability of violence declines. Third parties who are of moderately high status—as legal officials today are with respect to middle- and upper-class people—are generally popular with disputants, effective in settling their conflicts peacefully, and helpful in creating an ethic of nonviolence. Overall, then, there appears to be a **U**-curved relationship between third-party status and violence.[1]

## Status Patterns in Criminal Homicide

"Social status" is a person's or group's position in the social hierarchy. In Black's theoretical paradigm, social status or advantage or privilege (I use these terms interchangeably throughout this book) is a composite concept, made up of five kinds of status, each located in a dimension of social space: (1) vertical, (2) radial, (3) cultural, (4) normative, and (5) organizational (Black, 1976). People who kill and are killed tend to be of low social status on some or all of these dimensions, not just in the United States but in other countries as well.[2]

### Wealth

Stephanie and Chuck are poor, relying on welfare and the odd job to support themselves and her four children (two of whom are also Chuck's). They rent rather than own their apartments. In this they are representative of the great majority of the principals involved in homicide cases. Whether measured by income or accumulated wealth (Black, 1976: 16), killers and victims are usually of low vertical, or economic, status. Marvin Wolfgang (1958: 37), for instance, found that "90–95 percent of the offenders of either race" arrested by the police for homicide in Philadelphia 1948–1952 were "in the lower end of the occupational scale, or from the category of skilled workers down through the unemployed." Elsewhere, it is the same. After reviewing studies from Denmark, England, Finland, Italy, Mexico, South Africa, Sri Lanka, and the United States, Wolfgang and a colleague conclude that "the overwhelming majority of homicides and other assaultive crimes are committed by persons from the lowest stratum of a social organization" (Wolfgang and Ferracuti, 1967: 261). This conclusion remains valid, confirmed by more recent studies in, for instance, Canada, Australia, and the United States (Silverman and Kennedy, 1993: 10; Polk, 1994; Goetting, 1995).

Although they have not attracted as much research attention, homicide victims tend to be similarily economically disadvantaged (see, e.g., Kposowa et al., 1994). In Australia, for instance, while unskilled workers constitute about 15 percent of the labor force (i.e., the population aged fifteen and over), they represent about 42 percent of homicide victims (and 56 percent of offenders) in New South Wales, the most populous state. Conversely, in the same state only 1 percent of victims (and less than half of 1 percent of offenders) are professionals or managers, though those groups make up about 25 percent of the national labor force (Wallace, 1986: 38; Australian Bureau of Statistics, 1996: 132).

There seems to be only one study of homicide committed by higher-status individuals (Green and Wakefield, 1979). Because the authors had trouble finding cases, they had to rely on reports published in the *New York Times* in which the offender was middle or upper class (i.e., belonged to one of eight occupational categories [professionals, managers, etc.]). Reasoning that *Times* coverage was likely to be most complete for the New York metropolitan area, the authors counted how many cases the newspaper reported with middle- and upper-class offenders and then compared that number to the thirteen thousand homicide arrests the police made in the area during the study period 1955–1975. The number they found? Twenty.

The authors themselves acknowledge that their numbers are only approximations. The *Times* may have missed some cases, although since high-status people usually kill high-status victims and their deaths are the kind that generally get reported, it probably includes most high-status killings. Moreover, there would have to be an enormous amount of underreporting in the newspaper to erase the underlying differences. Hence, while their results are estimates, they probably reflect the true state of affairs: "Fewer than 1% of the homicides were committed by that portion of the population comprising 60% of the labor force and members of their immediate families (upper-class members), while more than 99% were committed by the remainder of the population" (1979: 175).

If homicide is linked to low economic status, it follows that the number of people occupying low-economic-status positions should predict the amount of homicide a group or society has. It does. In the United States, as the wealth of ethnic groups such as Jews, Irish, Italians, and Poles has increased, their homicide rates have decreased (see, e.g., Lane, 1997). Economic deprivation (i.e., poverty and inequality combined) is one of the best predictors of how much homicide cities, metropolitan areas, and states will have (Land et al., 1990).[3] Internationally too, the countries with the highest homicide rates have the greatest gap between rich and poor (see, e.g., Unnithan et al., 1994: chap. 7). As one reviewer of the evidence puts it: "Around the world, at every level of economic development, increasing equality goes hand in hand with lower risks of homicide" (James, 1995: 65).

Integration

Integration (radial status) refers to the degree to which a person or group participates in social activity, how integrated or marginal they are (Black, 1976: 48). A common measure of integration is employment. Killers and their victims are commonly unemployed. Stephanie and Chuck, for example, are.

In Canada in 1991, for instance, people accused of homicide were four times (42 percent), and their victims almost three times (27 percent), more likely to be unemployed than members of the adult population as a whole (10 percent) (Wright, 1992: 15, 12; International Labor Office, 1992: 602). In Australia, during 1991–1992, about two-thirds of offenders and one-half of victims whose employment status could be tracked were outside the paid work force compared to less than one-half (43 percent) of the population aged fifteen and over (Strang, 1993: 29–30, 25; Australian Bureau of Statistics, 1994: 173; see also Wallace, 1986: 39).[4]

Marriage is a second type of social integration, the absence of which predicts involvement in homicide. Thus, in the United States, single men, men who are divorced/separated or widowed, and men who live alone are all more likely to be victims of homicide (though the pattern for women may be the reverse) (Kposowa et al., 1994). Throughout U.S. history, settings with large populations of unmarried men, such as frontiers, mining towns, cattle towns, and inner-city minority enclaves, have experienced high rates of lethal conflict (Courtwright, 1996).

Age is an indirect indicator of marginality in modern societies. Teenagers and people in their early twenties are less likely to be consumed by a career-type job or burdened with family responsibilities than older people, and less strongly integrated into their natal families than younger people. Young adults also typically have the highest probability of killing and being killed (Landau and Drapkin, 1968: 42; Strang, 1993: 30, 22; Federal Bureau of Investigation, 1996: 16). Furthermore, U.S. cities that have higher rates of unattached black teenagers (i.e., not in the labor force or in school) have higher rates of black homicide (Shihadeh and Flynn, 1996).

## Cultural Status

Cultural status can be gauged in several ways, including the amount of education people receive and their participation in the culture of the majority (conventionality) (Black, 1976: 64, 67–68). Regardless of how it is measured, homicide offenders and victims tend to be of low cultural status. Thus, they are typically at the bottom of the educational hierarchy in terms of the number of years of formal schooling they have attained. The fact that neither Stephanie nor Chuck finished high school therefore does not make them exceptional. In Detroit, for example, individuals arrested for homicide and their victims are less likely to have completed high school than members of the population as a whole (Goetting, 1995). In Canada, three quarters (73 percent) of murder suspects in the period 1961–1990 had less than a grade-11 education (Silverman and Kennedy, 1993: 12). By contrast, in 1978–1979 (approximately halfway through the study period), only 40 percent of the population aged eighteen and over had not completed grade 12 (Statistics Canada, 1992: 145).[5]

The principals in homicide cases are also disproportionately members of cultural minorities. In Australia, Aborigines are many times more likely to commit and be victims of homicide than the rest of the population, thirteen and nine times respectively in 1991–1992, for example (Strang, 1993: 39–40). In Canada, it has been found that "while Native people make up approximately 3% of the total population, they accounted for 19% of suspects and 15% of victims in all homicide offenses over the 1974–1987 period" (Anonymous, 1989: 2; see also Silverman and Kennedy, 1993: chap. 8). Compared to native Germans, Turkish migrants were more than 3.5 times more likely, and Italian migrants one-third more likely, to commit homicide in Germany in the 1960s (Zimmermann, 1966 cited in Nettler, 1982: 49). In Israel 1950–1964, rates of homicide offending and victimization were more than six times greater among non-Jews (mostly Arabs) than among the majority Jewish population (Landau and Drapkin, 1968: 9–10). And in Sweden, citizens of foreign countries make up 5 percent of the population but 29 percent of convicted homicide offenders and 20 percent of their victims (Hofer, 1990: 33–34).

The same pattern is found in the United States: African Americans, like Chuck and Stephanie, are about five times more likely than members of the majority white population to be arrested for, or be a victim of, homicide (Reiss and Roth, 1993: 70–72). Native Americans are about twice as likely as whites to be homicide suspects or victims (Bachman, 1992: 12). (Latino probabilities are more difficult to estimate, but they appear to lie somewhere between those of African Americans and Native Americans [Martinez, 1996].) Moreover, the size of the black population strongly predicts homicide rates in cities, metropolitan areas, and states (see, e.g., Land et al., 1990: 928–930). Large Latino and Native American populations also appear to result in elevated rates of homicide (Kposowa and Breault, 1993).

Respectability

Respectability (normative status) is the degree to which a person or group has been free of social control in the past (Black,

1976: 111). Populations of homicide offenders and victims rank low on this dimension of status as well, and usually have higher-than-average rates of arrest and conviction for a variety of offenses. Stephanie, for example, has been arrested four times and convicted twice, once for drug possession and once for disorderly conduct. (I have no information on whether Chuck had a criminal record.) In the United States generally, the National Criminal Justice Commission estimates that about 30 million people have an arrest record (Donziger, 1996: 36). That represents approximately 15 percent of the population over sixteen years of age (calculated from Bureau of the Census, 1996: 15). Homicide studies reveal, however, that typically about 70 percent of offenders have been arrested in the past (usually more than once: Wolfgang, 1958: 177) and about 50 percent have been convicted of an offense (see Kleck and Bordua, 1983: 293). In Sweden, approximately 60 percent of people convicted of homicide have a prior criminal record for a serious crime (i.e., one resulting in more than a fine) compared to 2.5 percent of the general population (Hofer, 1990: 32, 40–41). In other countries, such as Australia and Canada, homicide offenders have similarly high arrest rates (Strang, 1993: 33; Wallace, 1986: 44–46; Wright, 1992).

Less is known about the criminal record of victims, but the same pattern is evident. In Wolfgang's (1958: 175, 180) study of 1948–1952 Philadelphia criminal homicide, almost half of the victims had a history of arrest. In Australia, about one-third of victims have a criminal history (Strang, 1993:27); in Canada, almost one-half do (Wright, 1992).[6]

## Organizational Status

Because there is very little information on the organizational affiliations of killers and victims, the fifth type of status—organizational status (Black, 1976: 92)—can be dealt with quickly. Like Stephanie and Chuck, most people today participate in homicide as individuals rather than as members of organized groups. But if the principals act as members of organized groups, they usually do so as members of low-status groups, such as street or prison gangs, rather than high-status groups, such as business corporations. So it too fits the pattern.

### Can We Trust the Statistics?

Although the statistics are consistent, they may be wrong. They are based primarily on arrests made by police, and experience has shown that when studies move away from police arrest data and draw instead on surveys in which people provide anonymous reports of their own criminal behavior (known as "self-report studies"), the correlation between low social status and crime/delinquency attenuates and sometimes even disappears (Tittle et al., 1978; Tittle and Meier, 1990).[7] Perhaps, then, more complete information would reveal that the reason that low-status people, like Stephanie and Chuck, show up more often in the police statistics is not because they kill and are killed more frequently but because the police monitor their actions more closely. After all, about one homicide in three in the United States currently does not result in an arrest (Federal Bureau of Investigation, 1996: 22). Maybe the elite are getting away with murder.

That is extremely unlikely. It is virtually certain that the unsolved homicides are not committed mainly by high-status people. Like other offenders, higher-status people tend to kill victims from the same social stratum as themselves (see Green and Wakefield, 1979). The killing of a high-status person—a wealthy businessman, for example—typically finds the police going to great lengths to locate the killer (see Cooney, 1994). Cases with low-status, not high-status, victims are therefore more likely to be unsolved. Furthermore, high-status people are unlikely to be departing from the norm by killing people lower in status than themselves with any frequency for several reasons. First, the United States has a considerable amount of residential segregation by class: the rich live with the rich and the poor with the poor. Yet homicide generally occurs among people who live in proximity to one another (see, e.g., Cooney, 1998). Second, to balance the known trend for homicide to be committed primarily by lower-status individuals, higher-status people would have to be killing lower-status victims in such large numbers that community activists, reporters, scholars, or even police—all of whom could have something to gain by uncovering a significant hidden pattern—would almost certainly have documented it by now. Third, higher-status people do not have to resort to homicide because they have other outlets—most notably law—for redressing grievances against those below them in the status hierarchy, a point developed shortly.

None of this means that higher-status people are never involved in lethal conflict. They are. Occasionally, a privileged citizen kills a spouse or sibling, a police officer kills a suspect, an outwardly respectable business person involved in organized crime kills a rival or enemy. Additionally, men—the higher-status gender—kill more than women (Daly and Wilson, 1988: chaps. 6–7). But these deviations only qualify and do not negate the general pattern.

Stephanie and Chuck's position in the lower echelons of society, then, makes them typical of most modern homicide offenders and victims. Although by no means all low-status people are involved in homicide, the great majority of those who kill and are killed today are of low social status.

## Elite Violence

The fact that violence tends to be largely confined to people at the bottom of the social pyramid is one of the most consistent findings in criminology, confirmed by numerous studies not just in the United States, but in all modern societies for which there is information. Yet it does *not* represent an iron law of human behavior. Homicide is largely confined to low-status people only under particular social conditions. In earlier and in structurally simpler societies, lethal interpersonal disputes could be found at all status levels, including the very top. Several examples follow.

## Feuding

Stateless societies are comparatively egalitarian (see, e.g., Fried, 1967). There are few status differences among people, and those that do exist are not sharp and pronounced. Even so, there are sometimes individuals who have more wealth or influence than others. Although the advantages enjoyed by these people are comparatively small, they nonetheless allow us to observe elite conflict behavior in inchoate form.

The leading individuals and families in stateless societies are often not shy about pursuing their conflicts violently. On the contrary, they are, if anything more involved in violent conflict, especially reciprocal violence or feuding, than those beneath them in the social hierarchy.[8] In highland Albania, for instance, where high-status kinship groups would typically seek to exact lethal vengeance following the killing of one of their members, "low-class families would accept blood money" (Hasluck, 1954: 239). And in northern Pakistan, a region sufficiently remote to be largely beyond the state's effective jurisdiction, a murder dispute between less powerful lineages will often be settled by the payment of compensation, but "among elite Pukhtun who have a claim to local leadership, a feud must be carried through to its bitter conclusion, which usually entails the ruin of all the participants" (Lindholm, 1982: 74–75).

Whether high-status people are more likely to perpetrate the killings that give rise to the feud in the first place is unclear. There are hints here and there that that is the case. For example, among the Tauade of Papua New Guinea, chiefs were especially likely to kill those who insulted or attacked them (Hallpike, 1977: 199; see also Barton, 1938: 282). What is clear is that several anthropologists, working in different parts of the globe, report that socially prominent people in stateless societies are more assertive than most in using lethal violence to avenge insults, injuries, and killings.

As the authority of the state develops, inequality generally increases and feuding declines. But feuding does not disappear overnight. In early or developing states reciprocal violence often overlaps with legal conflict. Under these circumstances, feuding is commonly found at or toward the top of the social hierarchy (see, e.g., Wallace-Hadrill, 1959). Even as late as the nineteenth-century, for example, it was often the leading individuals and families who were most deeply involved in Appalachian feuds (Blee and Billings, 1996).

### Brawling

Although feuding between noble families eventually declined, other forms of elite violence remained common for long afterward. Elites came to renounce violent conflict only gradually, as late-medieval England illustrates. English aristocrats of the period rarely show up as defendants in court records, unlike, say, their Venetian counterparts (Ruggiero, 1980: chap. 5). But as James Given (1977: 22) notes in his study of thirteenth-century English homicide that "if any group was able to avoid being named as accused of homicide . . . it was this one." Given (1977: 34) quotes one medieval historian of the period who wrote that "few self-respecting gentlemen passed through the hot season of youth without having perpetrated a homicide or two" (Tout, 1920: 5). Even allowing for some exaggeration, it is undoubtedly true that elite individuals often resorted to force in their disputes with one another. As late as the sixteenth century, for example, although feuding had largely disappeared from all but some outlying regions, nonetheless "a gentleman carried a weapon at all times, and did not hesitate to use it" (Stone, 1965: 224). One eminent historian argues that in the sixteenth and seventeenth centuries "because of the habit of wearing swords, homicide was as common among the upper classes as among the lower" (Stone, 1983: 25). Whether it was as common or not, elites were certainly impulsive and rash, quick to anger and take offense. Furthermore, their violence was not hidden and private but open and public. Often, it involved groups. In Elizabethan England, brawls between gangs of rival aristocrats and their retinues were a not uncommon sight in the streets of the major cities:

> In London itself the fields about the City and even the main arterial roads were continued scenes of upper-class violence. Bloody brawls and even pitched battles occurred in Fleet Street and the Strand. . . . It was in Fleet Street that there took place in 1558 the armed affray between Sir John Perrot and William Phelippes, supported by their retainers; in Fleet Street that John Fortescue was beaten up by Lord Grey and his men in 1573; in Fleet Street that Edward Windham and Lord Rich carried on their repeated skirmishes in 1578; in Fleet Street that Lord Cromwell got mixed up in an armed affray in 1596; in the Strand that Lord Grey and his attendants attacked the Earl of Southampton and his boy in 1600; in the Strand that Edward Cecil, future Viscount Wimbledon, lay in wait with ten soldiers to catch Auditor Povey. (Stone, 1965: 231–232)

Over time, public brawling of this kind disappeared. Eschewing collective affrays, elites began to adopt a more formal and individualistic type of violence: the duel.

### Dueling

The duel emerged in Italy in the fifteenth century, spread to France, was practiced by the elite all across Europe by 1700, and died out in the latter half of the nineteenth century. Notable for its formality, strict rules regarding, for instance, the use of weapons (first the rapier, later the épée, and later still the pistol) governed the practice. Their purpose was to give both parties an equal chance of prevailing. To ensure that the proper procedure was followed, the principals appointed third parties known as seconds, themselves typically gentlemen of some standing (Kiernan, 1988).

The list of high-status individuals known to have fought duels is impressive: when the British prime minister, the duke of

Wellington, dueled at the age of sixty in 1829 he was the sixth holder of that office in the previous one hundred years to do so; the Russian writers Pushkin (in 1837) and Lermontov (in 1841) both lost their lives to dueling; the composer Handel almost killed a conductor in an impromptu sword fight in 1704; and arguably the most influential Irish leader of the early nineteenth century, Daniel O'Connell, killed a political opponent in a duel in 1815 (Kiernan, 1988).

O'Connell is worth dwelling on briefly because his career nicely illustrates how easily a prominent public figure could become the regular target of dueling challenges. Born in 1775 to a well-to-do landowning family in the remote southwest corner of Ireland, O'Connell was not a member of the Protestant Anglo-Irish establishment, well known for its enthusiastic embrace of the dueling ethos. (A group of Anglo-Irish gentry, for example, authored an influential code of dueling known as the Twenty-six Commandments [Kiernan, 1988: 145].) But his rise to prominence as a high-earning London lawyer coupled with his public leadership of the Irish people (which included holding a seat in the British parliament) for more than twenty years put him among the elite of both Irish and English social circles. "The Liberator," as he came to be known, had a sharp tongue that angered his enemies and brought him to the brink of a duel on several occasions. Perhaps to quell the whispers of cowardice, he eventually took the field, having been challenged by a member of Dublin Corporation for calling the Corporation "beggarly" (Trench, 1984). After mortally wounding his challenger, he became opposed to the practice. His adversaries were not impressed by his new moral stand: "It galled many of those who suffered the lash of his lacerating tongue that they could not redeem their injured reputations in time-honoured fashion by means of a duel" (Kelly, 1995: 263). Political opponents, including the future prime minister Benjamin Disraeli, continued to try to call him out (Kiernan, 1988: 212). On more than one occasion, O'Connell was forced into the delicate task of arguing his way out of conflicts while still trying to maintain his own honor and that of the movement he represented. Far from his status repelling dueling challenges, O'Connell's position as a prominent, combative, and controversial political leader attracted them at a steady rate over the course of his entire career (Kelly, 1995: 242–247, 261–263).

As dueling became less frequent, it also became less lethal. But how many people died dueling and what percentage those deaths were of all homicides are questions that have never been answered and perhaps never will be (but see, e.g., Kelly, 1995). Because of the elevated rank of the participants, dueling probably attracted considerably more attention than violence among low-status people. For every aristocrat killed in a duel, it is likely that a significant number of commoners perished in brawls, vendettas, feuds, and arguments that have left few documentary traces. What is certain, however, is that because of dueling, lethal violence loomed larger in the social existence of the elite of early modern Europe than it does in the everyday life of better-off people today.

One of the last outposts of dueling culture was the nineteenth-century antebellum American South. Here again, only the social elite participated in formal duels (see, e.g., Wyatt-Brown, 1982: 368). Perhaps the most renowned high-status duelist was Andrew Jackson, who fought numerous times in the course of a life in which he held the office of judge, general, and president of the United States (Williams, 1980: 18–19). Other notable Southerners who dueled were Confederate States Vice-President Alexander Stephens, Mississippi governor and territorial delegate George Poindexter, and Senators Thomas Hart Benton and Henry Clay (Williams, 1980: 11–12). But "dozens of congressmen, several state governors, numerous newspaper editors and publishers, and a host of prominent planters were duelists" (Williams, 1980: 11).

## Lynching

After the Civil War dueling died out, but the participation of high-status southerners, albeit not of the same stature as before, in homicide did not. Lethal conflict now primarily took the form of lynching in which groups—usually white—killed individuals—usually black (although, as mentioned, there was also some feuding between elite white families in Appalachia [Waller, 1988; Blee and Billings, 1996]). Lynching is something of a marginal case because although local elites assumed leadership roles throughout the South, helping to organize and lead the lynching parties, they did not necessarily do the actual killing. Nonetheless, local southern elites undoubtedly played a part, sometimes a large one, in many lynchings (see, e.g., Brundage, 1993: 37–38; Tolnay and Beck, 1995: 15). For instance, in Caddo Parish, Louisiana, one of the most violent communities in the postbellum South, the three most common occupational categories involved in lynching from 1865 to 1876 were the comparatively high status ones of "planter," "farmer," and "professional" (Vandal, 1991).

This review of elite homicide is not intended to be exhaustive; the cross-cultural and historical literatures may well contain additional instances. However, in accounts of violence since the demise of lynching examples of higher-status homicide are increasingly sparse. The only consistent exceptions are those noted earlier. The participation of higher-status people in official, domestic, and organized crime killing can therefore be seen as atavistic remnants of a pattern once vastly more common.[9]

## Third-Party Social Status

Why, then, is there is so little high-status interpersonal homicide now compared to earlier and simpler societies? One thing is clear: the fact that modern middle- and upper-class people rarely kill one another is not because they lack conflict. Doctors and lawyers, entrepreneurs and accountants, civil servants and professors do not lead lives of total harmony. Conflict is part and parcel of the human experience, and high social standing does not insulate people from experiencing their share of disagreements and disputes. Nor are the privileged today slow to assert themselves in matters of conflict. In fact, high-status people are more likely to press their claims than are socially disadvantaged people. Where a poor or uneducated person might be slow to pursue a grievance against a corporation, for example, his or her wealthier or more educated counterpart is more likely to take legal action (Black, 1976: 24–28).

The answer can be found instead in the abstract idea of third-party social status. Third parties can be of higher, lower, or the same status as the principals. Violence is least likely when third parties, such as legal officials, are neither too high nor too low in status relative to the principals. Expressed in propositional terms, my argument is

> *The relationship between violence and third-party status superiority is U-curved.*

This proposition predicts that the probability of violence will be high when third parties are either considerably superior to the principals in status or inferior to them in status. Between these extremes—when the third party is moderately superior in status—the likelihood of violence declines.

### High-Status Third Parties

Black (1993b: chap. 8) argues that as third parties increase in status, their behavior changes along four dimensions. The higher the status of third parties—the greater their status superiority—the more *decisive* (i.e., likely to declare an outright winner rather than forge a compromise decision); *formalistic* (i.e., more oriented to explicit rules and less concerned with the equities of the case); *coercive* (i.e., willing to use force rather than persuasion); and *punitive* (i.e., a propensity to punish) they are toward the disputants. Thus, while third parties who are only slightly above the principals in status are likely to mediate an agreement between the disputants, third parties who are considerably superior in status are prone to adjudicate cases in a severe and unsympathetic, or, in Black's terms, moralistic, manner.

Disputants do not like moralistic third parties (Black, 1993b: 148). Given a choice, disputants prefer third parties who give a little to both sides, who respond not just to technical rules but to the equities of the case, who rely on the power of persuasion, and who do not seek to punish the losing party. If only moralistic third parties are available, disputants will often handle conflict on their own and eschew outside intervention. Third parties who are high above the parties in social status, then, often find their authority contested by low-status disputants. The ensuing struggle increases the likelihood that the disputants will use violence for two reasons. First, since third-party settlement is effectively unavailable, the disputants have fewer means of resolving their dispute peacefully. Settlement is not necessary for a peaceful outcome—the parties can negotiate an agreement, avoid one another, or tolerate their grievances—but it helps (see Horwitz, 1990: 128–131). Second, and more indirectly but perhaps even more importantly, with no third parties to settle disputes, disputants tend to develop a moral system that emphasizes self-reliance, toughness, and sensitivity to insult. Students of violence call this moral system honor and it is closely linked to high rates of lethal conflict. Chapter 5 analyzes honor in detail; here the emphasis is on the first, more direct effect of third-party status superiority.

To see the practical importance of third-party status, consider legal officials. Police officers, prosecutors, and judges largely derive their status from the state.[10] In modern society, the great wealth, integration, organization, conventionality, and respectability of the state make it the quintessential high-status institution. Legal officials are therefore closer in status—less status superior—to high-status citizens than to low-status citizens. Consequently, law tends to be nonrepressive and broadly acceptable to those who are wealthy, employed, married, educated, and without criminal records. When these groups have disputes, they can access lawyers and legal officials and expect to be treated in a nonmoralistic fashion by receiving an impartial and professional analysis of the issues dividing them. Low-status people, by contrast, consistently attract a sharper edge of the law—surveillance, arrest, prosecution, and punishment—causing many to turn away from the legal system and to substitute their own means of resolving disputes. Law is effectively unavailable to these socially disadvantaged groups, who must exist largely without the protection of the state.

More than three hundred years ago, Thomas Hobbes ([1651] 1909: 97) argued that in the absence of the state, violence will pervade social existence; life will be, to cite his famous phrase, "nasty, brutish, and short." Whether Hobbes was right in arguing that the development of the state reduces violence is discussed in the next chapter. But Hobbes's idea helps to explain violence within state societies. In a paper entitled "Crime as Social Control," Black (1983) gave Hobbesianism a new twist, proposing that some groups can be effectively stateless though they nominally live under the jurisdiction of a state. Drawing on his earlier theory of law, Black (1976) argued that the state's system of social control—law—flourishes among the wealthy, the integrated, the conventional, and the respectable, as well as among members of ethnic and racial majorities. Conversely, the poor, marginals, unconventionals, the unrespectable, and members of ethnic and racial minorities occupy what he termed stateless locations within modern state societies and hence are more likely to use aggressive tactics—fighting, burning, seizing, killing, and so forth—to resolve their conflicts. (To distinguish such societies from actual stateless societies, they might be called "virtual stateless" locations.) As we have seen, these are exactly the groups that generate the homicide statistics.[11]

Stephanie provides a tangible example of how status inferiority to the law results in virtual statelessness. Stephanie is adept at surviving in the harsh reality of poverty, unemployment, addiction, and violence in which she finds herself. (Her former husband, for example, killed a man in a robbery and received a seventy-six-year prison sentence.) Her skills are not much valued in the conventional world. When she leaves prison, Stephanie hopes to get "a good suit job, and a car." But like so many others from disadvantaged backgrounds, Stephanie's lack of credentials—educational and social—make these modest middle-class goals difficult to attain (Bourgois, 1995: chap. 4). She does not belong to the world of those who hand out jobs in business, government, and elsewhere, and this affects the way she has to deal with Chuck. While in theory the police and the courts are there for her protection, she knows that in practice their actions are unpredictable and, often, counterproductive. She does not speak the language of the law, see the point of many of its rules, or respect its involvement in her affairs or those of her community. Because of her low-status characteristics, she is, to the police, just another petty criminal from the ghetto. Why should they protect her? They are reluctant to intervene in disputes between intimates anyway (Black, 1976: 40–48). If they take any action, it will probably be to arrest Chuck. But that is just likely to make him angry with Stephanie. Far from being "scared straight," unemployed men, like Chuck, often become more domestically violent after being arrested for it (Sherman, 1992). Hence, if Stephanie does invoke the law against Chuck, she may well find that doing so backfires on her. She is unlikely to try it again. Distant as they are, legal officials cannot be trusted. She is on her own. She must protect herself.

## Low-Status Third Parties

But just as people will resist third parties who are too superior in status, so too they will reject third parties who are not superior enough. People tend to look only to those above them in the status hierarchy to settle disputes (Black and Baumgartner, 1983: 113). M. P. Baumgartner has put the point well:

> Where social stratification exists, there is generally an upward drift of disputes in which higher-status people are called upon to settle the affairs of those beneath them. . . . Submitting a conflict to third-party intervention (especially in its more coercive forms such as arbitration

and adjudication) entails a compromise of autonomy and a kind of subordination of the disputants to the outside party or parties involved. For this reason, high-status people often limit third-party involvement except under certain conditions. . . . For an individual to submit a . . . conflict . . . to a third party who is of no higher social standing than himself or herself is an act of deference at odds with social realities. (Baumgartner, 1988: 68–69)

Third parties who are not at least as high in social status as the principals will, therefore, tend to be ignored (see also Baumgartner, 1992: 23–25). People will not bring their disputes before them and will seek alternative ways of settling their conflicts. With third-party settlement once again effectively unavailable, disputes are more likely to attract violence for the same two reasons mentioned earlier: the principals have fewer peaceful options and are more likely to develop an ethic of honor.

The low relative status of third parties explains the patterns of elite violence discussed earlier. When no state exists at all, homicide is found throughout the social hierarchy because there are no state officials to whom people can be status inferior. Indeed, homicide is most likely at the highest status levels because when order is uncertain, social status depends in part on being able to protect one's self and one's family from enemies and predators: one cannot rely on the state to do it.

As the state develops, it only gradually begins to establish its position and to outrank higher-status individuals. In medieval and early modern Europe, few individuals or institutions could match the aristocracy in status. Aristocrats owned the wealth, made all important community decisions, and set the standards for moral, aesthetic, religious, and other forms of cultural expression; they were lords of the earth. But the very elevation of their social position meant that they had few status superiors to whom they could present their interpersonal conflicts. The state, after all, was of variable and uncertain status (see, e.g., Elias [1939] 1982). By modern standards, its resources were sparse and its ability to engage in collective action limited. In addition, its officers were few and its institutions, especially in the hinterland, weak. Aristocrats were unlikely to humble themselves by bringing their interpersonal disputes before a mere public servant, such as a local magistrate (Stone, 1965: 229–231).

Only as the state acquired more wealth and organizational capacity did its officers come to represent a body of undeniably high stature and elites come to accept that recourse to a court was compatible with their personal dignity. That took time; the state came up in the world gradually, slowly increasing its number of officers and institutions, extending its reach to the most remote corners of its territory, and securing enough wealth to fund an elaborate, permanent bureaucracy.

A single variable will rarely explain a complex pattern, however. A further reason that lynching is important is because it reveals the explanatory limitations of third-party status superiority. After the Civil War, the southern landed gentry suffered a significant decline in relative status. Conversely, while legal institutions and officials were initially few and far between in mountainous and remote regions, by the end of the nineteenth century, the legal system had a strong presence virtually everywhere (see, e.g., Ayers, 1984). Moreover, in a significant number of cases, the lynching group seized the alleged crime suspect from police custody before killing him. Law was clearly available in these cases (Senechal de la Roche, 1996: 105).

Even so, third-party status superiority explains the broad trend by which elite violence gradually became less frequent. Furthermore, the **U**-curved proposition provides an explanation of several other patterns of homicide, as the next chapter reveals.

To recapitulate: One of the concomitants of low social status in the modern world is increased exposure to violence, whether as offender or victim. Most homicide today occurs among the socially disadvantaged: the poor, the young, the unemployed, the less educated, those with criminal records, and members of racial and ethnic minorities. The privileged are largely immune to serious violence, rarely killing or being killed.

It was not always so. In earlier and simpler societies, violence occurred at all levels of status, among elites and nonelites alike. Perhaps the best known instance of elite violence is dueling, which flourished among aristocrats in Europe and their counterparts in America for several centuries. But dueling is far from being the only example of violent conflict among the socially privileged.

The explanation of these patterns lies with the social status of third parties relative to that of the principals—their status superiority. The overall relationship between violence and third-party status superiority seems to be **U**-shaped. Violence occurs when third parties are either too high in status (as legal officials are for socially disadvantaged disputants today) or not high enough in status (as legal officials were for elites in earlier societies). Between these poles—when third parties are of moderately superior status (as legal officials are for middle- and higher-status people today)—violence typically becomes less frequent.

Violence and peacefulness, it follows, are not written into people's genes but are products of their social conditions. Elites are not intrinsically peaceful in the prosecution of their conflicts; they are so only under the conditions prevailing within modern state societies. Remove third-party settlement—by, for example, making high-status people virtually or actually stateless—and violence will climb the social hierarchy. Conversely, low-status people are not inherently violent. Find ways of reducing the status gap between them and third parties and their lives ought to become more peaceful.

# 3

# The ∪-Curve of Violence 2

"My brother [/Twi] was killed southwest of No//o!kau. . . .
People said that /Twi was one who had killed too many people so they killed him with spears and arrows. He had killed
two people already, and on the day he died he stabbed a
woman and killed a man.

It was /Xashe who attacked /Twi first. He ambushed him
near the camp and shot a poisoned arrow into his hip. They
grappled hand to hand, and /Twi had him down and was
reaching for his knife when /Xashe's wife's mother grabbed
/Twi from behind and yelled to /Xashe, "Run away! This
man will kill everyone!" And /Xashe ran away.

/Twi pulled the arrow out of his hip and went back to his
hut, where he sat down. Then some people gathered and
tried to help him by cutting and sucking out poison. /Twi
said, "This poison is killing me. I want to piss." But instead
of pissing, he deceived the people, grabbed a spear, and
flailed out with it, stabbing a woman named //Kushe in the
mouth, ripping open her cheek. When //Kushe's husband
N!eishi came to her aid, /Twi deceived him too and shot him
with a poisoned arrow in the back as he dodged. And
N!eishi fell down.

Now everyone took cover, and others shot at /Twi, and
no one came to his aid because all those people had decided
he had to die. But he still chased after some, firing arrows,
but he didn't hit any more.

Then he returned to the village and sat in the middle. The
others crept back to the edge of the village and kept under
cover. /Twi called out, "Hey are you all still afraid of me?
Well I am finished, I have no more breath. Come here and
kill me. . . . Do you fear my weapons? Here I am putting

them out of reach. I won't touch them. Come kill me."
    Then they all fired on him with poisoned arrows till he
looked like a porcupine. Then he lay flat. All approached
him, men and women, and stabbed his body with spears
even after he was dead.                    (Lee, 1979: 394)

This account of homicide among the Ju/'hoansi of the
Kalahari desert (formerly known as the !Kung San) collected by
the anthropologist Richard Lee illustrates a problem that all
human societies must confront at some point: How can an in-
corrigibly violent person be rendered harmless? In state societies, the government bears the responsibility of removing the
dangerous from circulation by imprisonment, banishment, or
execution. In stateless societies, the task of containment falls on
ordinary people. They typically lack the overwhelming coercive
force of states and so will usually be less able to overpower violent deviants without further bloodshed. Thus, the Ju/'hoansi effort to overcome /Twi—who had already killed two people—
cost the life of one man and nearly that of a woman as well. Because states can more easily bring episodes or cycles of violence
to a halt, state societies might reasonably be thought to enjoy
generally lower rates of violence. On the other hand, it is possible that the sheer scale and anonymity of state societies generate
more violence that must be contained. A third possibility is that
the state is not all that important and has no real effect on levels of violent conflict.

    This chapter addresses the issue of whether the state in fact
curtails violence within societies. Consistent with the argument
that there is a **U**-curved relationship between third-party status superiority and violence, the answer proffered is a heavily
qualified yes. The advent of the state usually reduces violence
in places in which it was frequent. But settings with developed
systems of informal third-party settlement will often have low

levels of violence to begin with and so the addition of a state will not serve to decrease violent conflict and may even increase it. Moreover, if the state is accompanied by pronounced status inequality, an ethic of oppositional honor (discussed in chapter 5) may arise that elevates rates of violence. The presence of third parties of moderately superior social status, not the state as such, appears to be the crucial variable in securing low rates of violent conflict.[1]

## Violence in Stateless Societies

Cross-cultural anthropologists define a society in linguistic terms: "A society is a more less continuously distributed population that speaks a common language" (Ember and Ember, 1994: 621). (Because states often incorporate more than one society, many modern countries have more than one society or culture in this sense.) A state may be defined as "an autonomous political unit, encompassing many communities within its territory and having a centralized government with the power to collect taxes, draft men for work or war, and decree and enforce laws" (Carneiro, 1970: 733).

Do state societies have more homicide than societies in which people are actually stateless? In the absence of a state, are societies always internally violent? Scholars have long pondered these questions, often coming to conflicting conclusions.

### The Amount of Homicide

Hobbes provided an early and eloquent statement of the argument that without the state, life is unbearably violent:

> [I]t is manifest that during the time men live without a common power to keep them all in awe, they are in that condition which is called Warre; and such a warre, as is of every man, against every man.                                           ([1651] 1909: 96)

The consequences of warre are

> continuall feare, and danger of violent death; And the life of man,
> solitary, poore, nasty, brutish, and short.            ([1651] 1909: 97)

The solution is sovereign power "as great, as possibly men can be imagined to make it" ([1651] 1909: 160).

Not everybody agrees with Hobbes. Some argue, for example, that the state has no impact on the incidence of violence one way or the other. The anarchist theorist Peter Kropotkin expressed one version of this idea as follows:

> [T]he severity of punishment does not diminish the amount of crime. Hang, and if you like, quarter murderers, and the number of murders will not decrease by one. On the other hand, abolish the penalty of death, and there will not be one murder more; there will be fewer. Statistics prove it. But if the harvest is good, and bread cheap, the weather fine, the number of murders immediately decreases. This again is proved by statistics. The amount of crime always augments and diminishes in proportion to the price of provisions and the state of the weather."[2]            ([1886] 1975: 42)

Although Hobbes's view is the dominant one, the question of whether he is right has never been fully resolved. Note that Hobbes states his case very strongly, so that even a single stateless society with a low rate of violence would refute it. Is there, then, a properly documented example of a stateless society in which people rarely or never kill one another?

The "properly documented" qualification is necessary because experience has shown that reports that societies are peaceful cannot always be taken at face value. Preindustrial people may be reluctant to discuss the subject of killing, with the result that even careful ethnographers can fail to find any evidence of it. Richard Lee (1979: 382) recounts that he was in the field a full fourteen months among the Ju/'hoansi before they told him anything about their lethal conflict. His interest aroused, he pursued the subject, learning, over the next two years, of a total of twenty-two homicides committed between 1920 and 1970. In a population of just fifteen hundred people that represents a significant amount of lethal conflict, certainly enough to contradict reports by previous anthropologists that the Ju/'hoansi are non-violent.

Even taking this caution into account, however, the strong version of Hobbes is wrong. There are several examples of non-violent stateless people (see, e.g., Turnbull, 1961, 1965, 1978). One well-documented case is the Semai, a group of about thirteen thousand people who live deep within the rain forest of the central Malay Peninsula in small bands rarely exceeding one hundred people (Dentan, 1978, 1979, 1988; Robarchek, 1977; Robarchek and Dentan, 1987). Although nominally part of the Malayan state, the geographical isolation of the Semai (at least at the time they were studied) means that they are politically self-governing. Each band has its own well-defined territory and a headman whose authority is based on persuasion, not coercion. To survive, the Semai carve gardens out of the forest, planting rice and manioc. They supplement their crop diet with game that they hunt with blowpipes, poisoned darts, and a variety of small snares. Every few years as the soil and game are depleted, they abandon their old gardens and create new ones. Theirs is a simple existence, and a peaceful one too. As one summary puts it, "[P]hysical violence of any sort is extremely uncommon; adults do not fight, husbands do not beat their wives nor parents their children, and homicide is so rare as to be virtually nonexistent" (Robarchek and Robarchek, 1992: 192).

A second example is the Cheyenne Indians of the Great Plains of North America. For most of the nineteenth century, the Cheyenne were equine hunters and gatherers. Although they counted among their numbers many hot-headed young warriors who regularly raided and battled other tribes, the Cheyenne succeeded in keeping intratribal homicide within reasonable boundaries. Over a forty-five-year period (1835–1879) they had some sixteen homicides, giving them an annual rate of approximately 10 per 100,000, about the same rate as the United States today (Llewellyn and Hoebel, 1941: 132). While this might initially seem quite high, remember that it comes from a society lacking the benefit of modern emergency medical care so that many wounds that today could be treated would then have proved fatal. (In general, because of differences in weaponry and medical knowledge, care should be exercised in comparing homicide rates across societies at different stages of technological and scientific development. Numbers and rates should not be given too much weight.)

The reasons for the absence of violence among the Semai and the low level among the Cheyenne will be considered a little later. The point for now is that the Cheyenne clearly contradict the idea that stateless societies are always more violent than modern state societies, while the Semai show that they can, in fact, be extremely peaceful (see also Howell and Willis, 1989).

### Cross-Cultural Studies

But while stateless societies are not always violent, it is possible that they usually are. So although Hobbesianism cannot be supported in its strongest form, it may be that a weaker version is more defensible. In this weaker version, the state would be but one factor that affects violence. If correct, it would mean that homicide rates, for instance, in stateless societies are higher on average than in state societies, even though particular stateless societies may have very little killing. Hobbes himself gives some support to this weaker version of his thesis: "It may peradventure be thought, that there was never such a time, nor condition of warre as this; and I believe it was never generally so, over all the world" ([1651] 1909: 77).

To a modern social scientist, this weaker version is considerably more plausible because one-variable explanations of complex phenomena such as violence almost never work. Moreover, it seems reasonable to suggest that legal institutions settle some conflicts that would otherwise be pursued with violence. However, to test the weaker version adequately we would need to know how high homicide rates are in general in stateless as compared to state societies. We lack that information. Our knowledge is especially incomplete for societies that do not have a state. Valuable though the cross-cultural record is, anthropologists have been able to study only a tiny percentage of all the stateless societies that have ever existed (and those under less-than-pristine conditions). Moreover, even when they have been able to work with stateless groups, the information they have obtained on violence is often tantalizingly incomplete.

Cross-cultural studies using large samples (usually of at least thirty societies) are therefore of less assistance than one might suppose. In general, however, these studies support the idea that the state or, more generally, judicial and political development, lowers rates of violence. One study, for instance, found that societies with greater political centralization have less dyadic conflict management than societies with less political centralization (Koch and Sodergen, 1976). Because dyadic conflict management in the societies sampled nearly always consists of violent self-help (1976: 452), the analysis in effect shows that the presence of more centralized political institutions reduces violence. Another study reports that more developed judicial and, especially, political authority results in less socially unapproved homicide (Rosenfeld and Messner, 1991). And a third study found, most directly, that rates of lethal violence are negatively correlated with third-party arbitration and adjudication (Masumura, 1977).

Other studies provide more equivocal support. Analyses of feuding and internal war (i.e., violence between political communities within the same society) found that political centralization reduces both forms of violence only under certain conditions (Otterbein and Otterbein, 1965; Otterbein, 1968). For example, more centralized societies have less feuding only if they are involved in external warfare. A final study reports that conflict internal to societies, including violence, is negatively, though weakly, related to the concentration of political power (Ross, 1993: 98).

All of these studies have limitations, however.[3] The analysis of dyadic conflict, for example, assumed that each society has a dominant mode of conflict management, an assumption that the authors acknowledge is empirically suspect in light of the fact that people in all societies handle their disputes in a variety of ways. Most important, the anthropological literature does not yield good measures of the amount of violence for large samples of societies. Hence, cross-cultural studies must rely on relatively broad and imprecise categories. In the feuding study, for instance, feuding was deemed to be "frequent" if the victim's kin were expected to take vengeance for a killing. But people often fail to do what is expected of them, especially when the expected behavior is personally risky. Moreover, as some evidence (to be discussed shortly) shows very clearly, the state may reduce violence considerably yet rates of violence remain "frequent."

## The Advent of the State

One of the difficulties of comparing state and nonstate societies is that the state is only one of many differences that might affect the incidence of violence. This is especially true when the comparison is between stateless preindustrial and modern state societies (see, e.g., Ember et al., 1992). While modern states generally have low rates of homicide (see, e.g., Reiss and Roth, 1993), those rates might be low because of factors such as increased interdependence between people (Durkheim, 1893: bk. 1; Elias, [1939] 1982; Black, 1993a: 47). Perhaps modern societies have comparatively little violent conflict for reasons that have nothing to do with the state.

A different kind of comparison—of the same society before and after the advent of the state—suggests, however, that some portion of the reduced rates of violence experienced by societies today should be credited to the state (see also, e.g., Tilly, 1990: 68–70). In many regions of the world, the first contact people had with a state was through colonialism. Colonial states systematically and vigorously suppressed indigenous violence (see, e.g., Middleton, 1965: 48; Sorenson, 1972; Harner, 1972: 210; Hart and Pilling, 1979: 83 n. 3; Pilling, 1968; Rodman and

Cooper, 1979; Boehm, 1984: 6–7; Chagnon, 1988; Heider, 1991: 96, 160).[4] By and large, suppression was effective and violence declined in those colonial territories that had experienced much of it. For example, after the advent of the colonial Australian administration, the Fore of highland New Guinea increasingly brought their conflicts before patrol officers for settlement, and a new "antifighting ethic quickly spread throughout the region" (Sorenson, 1972: 362).

Once again, this evidence must be interpreted cautiously. When a stateless society comes under the jurisdiction of a state, it often experiences a series of other changes as well, changes that might be more responsible for the reduction in lethal violence (e.g., access to Western medicine). Here the case of the Gebusi of New Guinea is particularly valuable because it presents an unusually pure case of state imposition. Except for a brief period of wage labor, virtually the only contact the Gebusi have had with Western culture has been with government patrols. At the time Knauft conducted his research in the early 1980s, their subsistence, settlement, and cultural patterns remained largely unchanged by contact: they had no leadership, specialization, stores, missions, or clinics; spoke only their own language; and did not migrate from their communities to seek employment (1985: 12–16). The experience of the Gebusi therefore represents something of a natural experiment on the relationship between the state and homicide, for the Gebusi did have a considerable amount of homicide, most of it the killing of people revealed through supernatural means to have, themselves, killed others through sorcery. Killings were carried out by a group of people led by the deceased person's closest kin. Knauft (1985: 116) summarizes the impact of the arrival of the state on this form of lethal conflict:

> The rate of homicide has decreased gradually since contact, from a high of 39.0 percent (97/249) of all adult deaths in the pre-contact era (c. 1940–1962) to 23.3 percent (24/103) during the period of Australian administration (1963–1975), and to 19.0 percent (8/42) under the national administration of Papua New Guinea (1975–

> 1982). The possibility of a five- to ten-year prison term for willful murder is clearly recognized by Gebusi as a cause of this decline, though the beliefs and motives that underlie homicide are unaffected by outside cultural influences. (1985: 116)

Note that the state did not just reduce Gebusi homicide in the short-term but did so for at least twenty years (i.e., until Knauft finished his field work in 1982). Note further that despite the introduction of the state, Gebusi homicide rates remained extremely high, thereby supporting the idea that the state is but one factor influencing violent conflict.

The Gebusi case, along with other anthropological evidence, suggests, then, that Hobbes put his finger on something important: when violence is common, the advent of the state can reduce violence. Even so, that statement is subject to several significant qualifications. One is that changes that accompany the advent of a modern state may increase violence. These changes might be called contact effects.

Contact Effects

Coming into contact with a state society is not necessarily a benign experience. Far from it. Contact with state powers has sometimes had catastrophic effects on stateless people, effects that include outright slaughter (see, e.g., Kroeber, 1961). All over the globe, preindustrial groups have been attacked and even eliminated following contact with technologically more developed societies (Bodley, 1990: chap. 3). In the usual scenario, the stateless people own land or resources valued by outsiders who enjoy the protection of a state (see, e.g., Beckerman and Lizarralde, 1995). The struggle that ensues is bloody but, in view of the disparity of sheer force, ultimately one-sided.

Although the devastation of this process can scarcely be overstated, the effect of coming into contact with a state society must be distinguished from the narrower effect of coming under the jurisdiction of a state. The lethal violence stateless people expe-

rience in these circumstances is usually attributable to the conflict following contact over land, minerals, or other resources
rather than the arrival of state jurisdiction. Once the issue of
asset ownership is settled, the state typically exerts its authority
by prohibiting violence if only better to exploit the indigenous
people. Contact with a new social world, a world that may be
extremely harsh and expropriative, not the advent of the state as
such, appears to be the cause of the violence.

There are other ways in which contact effects can stimulate
violence short of outright slaughter. A stateless society discussed
earlier—the Ju/'hoansi—provides a good illustration. Traditionally, the Ju/'hoansi (or !Kung San, as they used to be known)
hunted and gathered in the remote Kalahari desert of southern
Africa. Although they nominally fell under the jurisdiction of
the state of Botswana, their remoteness and isolation made them
effectively sovereign. Living in small, highly equal, nomadic
bands, they had no political leaders and no settlement agents—
no chiefs or elders before whom they brought disputes. They
were not an especially violent people, but, as we have seen,
homicide was by no means unknown among them either.

In 1946, a Ju/'hoansi man killed a member of a neighboring
farming group. The government responded by appointing a
headman to hear disputes in the region. After that, the number
of homicides declined:

> Since Isak became headman, !Kung have preferred to bring serious
> conflicts to him for adjudication rather than allow them cross the
> threshold of violence. The *kgotla* ("court") has proved extremely
> popular with the !Kung. . . . The reason for the court's popularity is
> not hard to find: it offers the !Kung a legal umbrella and relieves
> them of the heavy responsibility of resolving serious internal conflict
> under the threat of retaliation.
>
> (Lee, 1979: 396; see also Draper, 1978: 48–49)

To this point, then, the Ju/'hoansi are similar to the Gebusi in
that the arrival of the state reduced homicide among them. But
the story does not end there. Further contact with Western cul-

ture increased Ju/'hoansi homicide again. Elizabeth Marshall Thomas (1994), another anthropologist, recorded only six homicides among the Ju/'hoansi group she studied during their hunting-gathering period. But when she returned twenty years later, the Ju/'hoansi had given up their nomadic existence, attached themselves to the fringes of villages and towns, and experienced considerably more violent conflict. At least twenty of the two hundred people she had known have become victims of the lethal violence of other Ju/'hoansi, usually inflicted in the course of drunken arguments.

Several factors appear to be responsible for the increase in homicide, but one of the most important is that since contact the Ju/'hoansi have been proletarianized, they have become "the poorest of the poor," dependent on others for their survival (Thomas, 1994: 79). The Ju/'hoansi are now a dependent, low-status, minority group within a larger state society, a structural position that, as we have seen, is commonly associated with elevated rates of homicide.[5]

The Ju/'hoansi case shows, then, how contact with Western society may increase lethal conflict even as contact with a Western state reduces it. Although the state itself may lower rates of homicide, the state can be part of a larger package of contact changes that has the aggregate effect of raising them. The net result may be more rather than less homicide after the advent of the state.[6]

### Violence by and against the State

A second qualification to the idea that the state reduces violence is that, under certain conditions, the state itself is violent or attracts violence. As the status gap between the state and its citizens grows wider, lethal violence by (execution) and against (rebellion) the state becomes frequent (Black, 1993b: chap. 8; see also Durkheim, [1899–1900] 1969; Wittfogel, 1957; Rummel, 1995). Execution and rebellion are not "homicide" as defined in these pages, but they must be addressed, at least briefly, if a distorted picture of the relationship between the state and violence is not to be presented.

In noncentralized regimes, like modern democracies, the state is clearly superior to even the highest-status individual in status. But the status gap between the state and the citizen body is generally moderate, if only because the citizenry has considerable influence over state decisions through elections, judicial action, and other mechanisms. In somewhat more centralized regimes, the status gap increases as states concentrate decision making in a few hands and exert strong control over the activities of the populace. The status superiority of the state reaches its apogee in highly centralized states, such as empires and dictatorships. Controlling virtually all of the wealth in their societies, these states are organizationally vast, dominate every major social institution (e.g., family, economy, education, workplace), dictate cultural life, and actively promote their own reputation for good conduct in slogans and pronouncements.

Political violence generally increases with the status superiority of the state. Noncentralized regimes, like modern democracies, have very little political killing (Rummel, 1995). Semicentralized regimes, however, tend to experience a considerable amount of political rebellion (see, e.g., Muller, 1985; Boswell and Dixon, 1990). Highly centralized states have relatively little rebellion (or homicide) but a lot of execution. Compared to their noncentralized counterparts, for instance, centralized preindustrial polities have a longer list of offenses for which people can be executed (Otterbein, 1986).

The highly centralized states of the twentieth century killed enormous numbers of people. In a series of publications, the political scientist R. J. Rummel (1990, 1991, 1992, 1994) has undertaken the difficult task of estimating the number of people killed by governments in the period from 1900 to 1987. Rummel calculates that the German state killed more than 20 million European citizens during 1939–1945. This translates into an annual rate of 1,008 per 100,000 (i.e., about one hundred times greater than the homicide rate of the United States in the 1990s). During the Japanese occupation of China, Korea, Indonesia, Burma, and elsewhere in Asia in the years 1937–1945, he estimates, almost 6 million people were killed, yielding an annual rate of 999 per 100,000 (1992: 20–21). For Cambodia under the Khmer Rouge regime of 1975–1979, his estimate is 2 million or 8,160 per 100,000 (1994: 194).[7] These rates are calculated over a short period of time and hence are inflated. But his estimate for communist China of 120 per 100,000 (35 million victims in total) is based on thirty-eight years (1949–1987) (1991: chap. 8). And, most striking of all, is his estimate for the Soviet Union of 450 per 100,000, based on seventy-one years (62 million) (1917–1987) (1990: chap. 1).[8]

The central factor in explaining this killing, Rummel (1994) argues, is the degree of unrestrained power, or centralization, of the state. The more centralized the state, the higher its rate of execution, even after other relevant factors are controlled (e.g., social diversity, culture, and socioeconomic development) (Rummel, 1995). Thus, large-scale execution is rare in democracies, frequent in semicentralized regimes, and extremely common in centralized states.

There is more. Centralized states also lose a greater number of people in war with other states than their less centralized counterparts. Rummel (1994: 15) reports that the percentage of the population killed in twentieth-century wars is more than twice as high in centralized, as compared to democratic, regimes.

To summarize: Hobbes argued that the state reduces homicide. His argument in its strongest form is false because some stateless societies have little or no homicide to begin with. However, there is some evidence to suggest that the advent of the state reduces homicide, at least when homicide rates are high. But even this weaker version is subject to some important provisos: very strong or centralized states are extremely violent (even though they do not have much homicide between citizens), and contact with a state society may bring changes that result in increased homicide rates for some groups. Moreover, the next section documents a further qualification.

## Informal Settlement

Recall that the state's system of social control—law—is just one type of third-party settlement. Settlement can be much more informal, conducted by family members, friends, neighbors, or community leaders. Informal settlement usually takes the form of mediation in which the third party facilitates an agreement between the principals, or arbitration in which the third party devises a solution to the conflict but lacks the power to enforce it (see Black and Baumgartner, 1983). Whatever form it assumes, informal settlement has much the same effect as law, reducing the likelihood of violence among the principals. Law has always attracted much more scholarly attention, but its peace-enhancing properties are not unique.

### Societies with and without Settlement

To see the effect of the presence or absence of informal third-party settlement, consider three stateless societies that anthropologists have studied at first hand. The first two—the Semai and the Cheyenne—have already been described earlier as examples of societies with low levels of violence.

Although the Semai are largely equal among themselves, they do have a position of authority. Each hamlet has its own headman, one of whose duties is to provide a forum for hearing disputes, known as a *bcaraa'*. Held at the headman's house, a *bcaraa'* is attended by the principals, all their relatives, and anybody else who is interested. The principals and their supporters argue their case in detail, giving their version of the facts, recounting the history of the dispute, and raising every issue they think has any bearing on the dispute. Everybody has his or her say. Finally, when all concerned are simply too exhausted to add anything more—often this is two or three days later—the headman articulates the consensus that has emerged about the rights and wrongs of the affair. The *bcaraa'* usually concludes with the headman's imposing a small fine, and with admonitions by the headman and elders of the two kin groups about the necessity of avoiding the undesirable behavior in the future and the need for group harmony (Robarchek, 1977). The Semai, it will be recalled, are one of the most peaceful societies ever observed.

The success of the Cheyenne in restricting violent conflict in a society bristling with warriors provides a second instructive example. Each Cheyenne extended family had a headman. Above the headmen was the Council of Forty-four peace chiefs. Chiefs were men of high standing: they were comfortably off, participated in the affairs of the community, and had a reputation for integrity. Chiefs served for a period of ten years and appointed their own successors. They were expected to conduct themselves according to the strictest moral standards because in them was vested the supreme legislative, executive, and judicial authority of the tribe. The chiefs made policy, established rules, and settled cases. While their decisions could be penal in nature, they usually had a conciliatory dimension as well. For instance, if somebody did kill a fellow Cheyenne, the Council expelled him from the tribe, but not permanently; the Council reinstated the killer after a period of some years. Overall, the Council was remarkably adept at providing guidance and resolving disputes in a manner that promoted harmonious cooperation among a people accustomed to regular warfare (Llewellyn and Hoebel, 1941).

## The Waorani

If the Semai and Cheyenne illustrate the power of third-party settlement without law, the Waorani demonstrate what can happen when a society lacks all forms of settlement (Robarchek and Robarchek, 1992). The Waorani were traditionally a group of swidden gardeners and farmers thinly spread through a large section of the remote equatorial rain forest of the Ecuadorian Amazon. Highly egalitarian, the Waorani had no significant status distinctions of any kind. They also had one of the highest percentages of mortality from violence ever recorded. Drawing on extensive genealogical investigation, James Yost (1981) calculated that in the previous five generations almost half of all adult deaths (44 percent) were the result of internal violence. To put this in perspective: in the United States, which has considerably more criminal homicide than most industrialized countries, only about one death in one hundred is caused by homicide (calculated from Bureau of the Census 1996: 94).

The Waorani do not seem to have enjoyed their violent life very much. They made repeated attempts to stop it but failed; their divisions were too deep and grudges too intense for peace treaties to endure. A major stumbling block was that they lacked third-party settlement: Nobody had the standing or authority to bring warring parties together and to propose and monitor peaceful resolutions of conflict.

Waorani violence ended on a large scale only after the arrival of external third parties. In the late 1950s, a group of missionaries contacted the Waorani and made the cessation of violence their highest priority. They flew over Waorani settlements and dropped food, clothes, and other gifts to the people below. Then, using loudspeakers, they had Waorani from other groups talk to the groups on the ground and promise an end to feuds. Eventually, the missionaries would land and establish contact. Escape from the cycle of lethal vengeance soon followed.

The missionaries did not so much mediate particular conflicts as seek to end the violence altogether. They provided the necessary bridge between feuding factions, allowing them to give up violence without fear of being annihilated. Violence still occurs among the Waorani, but at nothing like its former level. Note that this sharp reduction was achieved without any help from the state. The missionaries' peacemaking owed nothing to coercion and everything to persuasion.

There are several reasons that the Waorani did not have indigenous settlement and the Semai and other groups did, some of which are explored in the next chapter. But one factor is that the Waorani did not have any positions of authoritative leadership, whereas the Semai had the position of headman (Robarchek and Robarchek, 1992: 196, 193). Semai headmen are only slightly higher in status than their fellow villagers, but the difference is enough to grant them the moral authority to intervene in and help settle the disputes of others, and more indirectly, to create an ethos of nonviolence. It does not take much status superiority to foster settlement and to inhibit violence.

### Comparing Legal and Informal Settlement

The argument, then, is that either informal or state-based third-party settlement can reduce violence. But which is more important? Is a stateless society with well-developed informal settlement going to experience less or more violence than a state society with few or no informal settlement mechanisms?

As always when dealing with the imperfect anthropological record, definitive answers to these questions are hard to come by. Nevertheless, it is possible to isolate some of the principal advantages (from the perspective of reducing violence) of each system.

States probably have an edge over their informal counterparts when it comes to dealing with that small minority of intractably violent people (like the incorrigible /Twi in the case described at the beginning of the chapter) who crop up at one time or another in virtually every society. Because states can summon greater force, they can more easily overwhelm and contain individuals who persistently endanger the lives of those around them. The importance of this factor, however, will vary with number of truly dangerous people in the population.

The coerciveness of the state also affects the way it handles conflicts between ordinary people not especially prone to violence. The state can compel these disputants to appear before judges and magistrates who will adjudicate the legal merits of their case. If necessary, the state will force the parties to comply with its ruling, even if they both disagree strongly with it. By contrast, the greater equality that generally underlies informal settlement renders it less coercive and its success more dependent on the consent of the principals. When people are comparatively equal, third parties lack the authority either to intervene in disputes against the wishes of the principals or to mandate a settlement not desired by them. If the principals are determined to fight there is not much outsiders can do to stop them.

The greater coerciveness of state settlement may not, however, actually contain violence more successfully. State coercion can alienate people, making them resentful of state authority and determined to resist it. Moreover, while informal settlement may be noncoercive, it is often backed by the moral authority of the community (e.g., the Semai *bcaraa'*). Disputants may well find it harder to disobey the consensus of informal tribunals than the mandates of judges and police officers.

A more consistent advantage enjoyed by states is that they typically have broader jurisdiction than informal systems of settlement. Informal social control is usually quite localized; it tends to apply to relatively small territories and restricted groups of people, and often does not encompass a whole society. Within its jurisdiction, settlement operates, but outside it, people must handle conflicts in other ways. Consequently, a comparatively small number of individuals can benefit from the peace-promoting activities of the third-party settlement. Law, on the other hand, is capable of affecting a much wider variety and number of groups located in many more areas. The large bureaucratic structure of the state allows it to distribute its officers and institutions throughout a broad territory and bring a large population within the same system of social control.

Despite its extensive jurisdiction, the state has some limitations as a violence-reducing mechanism. As we saw in the previous chapter, when status inequality grows, people at the bottom of the social hierarchy become distant from the state, develop a hostile relationship with it, and often reject state intervention in their affairs. Moreover, reliance on the state to settle conflict may cause indigenous forms of conflict management (including informal settlement) to atrophy (Black and Baumgartner, 1980; Black, 1989: chap. 5). For both reasons, the state may actually stimulate violence.

In informal systems, the status gap between third parties and principals is usually not that great. This, it may be recalled, has two effects, one direct, the other indirect. The direct effect is that people are quicker to turn to the system of informal settlement to resolve disputes they might otherwise prosecute violently. The indirect effect is that third-party settlement is not highly moralistic and so people do not develop a culture of honor in opposition to it. Together, the two effects serve to curtail the incidence of violent conflict.

In sum, theoretical arguments do not yield a decisive answer to the question of whether the state or informal settlement is more effective in reducing violence, and in the absence of empirical data, the issue must remain open. What does appear to be true is that settings that lack either a state or informal settlement are prone to violence, often on a considerable scale. Conversely, settings that have both the extensive jurisdiction of the state and the relative equality of informal settlement are likely to enjoy a considerable degree of peace.

## Informal Settlement Today

Informal settlement has by no means died out. Today, family members, friends, neighbors, supervisors, and others may be called on to settle disputes. But some groups may have little or no informal third-party settlement, and that can elevate their rate of violent conflict.

Low-income, urban, African-American communities are an example. Informal settlement appears to have declined in these communities at the same time that police data show that rates of homicide have increased within them (see, e.g., Hawkins, 1986). Elijah Anderson (1990) has described the loss of authority in urban black communities of the traditional "old head," a man or woman integrated into family and work life who commanded respect locally. Although rarely rich or famous, old heads enjoyed status on a number of dimensions: they were employed, of comfortable means, married, and involved in their communities. Traditionally, they dispensed advice to younger people, encouraged them to find employment, and served as models of the life attainable by hard work and law-abidingness. Although Anderson does not address their settlement role in any detail, he (1990: 69) does mention that old heads "preached anticrime and antitrouble messages," suggesting that informal dispute settlement was one service they routinely provided. If they did, they do so no longer. As manufacturing jobs have declined in number and stability, old heads have lost much of their prestige. The model they provide is outmoded and they themselves are either retired, unemployed, or "hanging on to residual manufacturing jobs" (1990: 242). Their much-reduced status has left a void, for without them younger people have available to them one less nonviolent means of settling their conflicts.[9]

Mention of low-income African-American communities leads back, once again, to Stephanie's case, described at the beginning of chapter 2. Apart from being virtually stateless because of the status superiority of the law, Stephanie did not have any informal system of settlement available to her either. She could, perhaps, have gone to a marriage counselor to try to resolve her problems with her partner, but that would have probably meant revealing her and Chuck's heroin habit. She could have looked for someone in the community to mediate their persistent conflicts, but, as Anderson reports, there are few suitable "old heads" or other people who have the stature to intervene in other people's affairs. No, she had to deal with her violent partner herself.

Stephanie's case, then, illustrates both parts of the U-shaped relationship. For her, legal officials are too vertically superior and informal third parties are not vertically superior enough. She and Chuck have to get by on their own the best they can; their fights and his death are the result.

In summary, social theorists have long discussed the Hobbesian question: Does the state make life within human communities less violent? The anthropological evidence reveals that the state is not, in fact, necessary to achieve low rates of violence. Societies that have extensive informal third-party settlement are largely peaceful, even without a legal system. Moreover, the state can itself be extremely violent. On the other hand, societies that lack a developed system of informal settlement may experience a lot of violent conflict that the advent of a state (or informal settlement) can reduce. In short, contrary to Hobbesian theory, the critical factor is not the form of third-party settlement but the presence or absence of third parties of moderately superior status.

The state and informal settlement each have distinctive advantages and disadvantages in curtailing violent conflict. The state increases the number of people subject to the same jurisdiction. But the fact that the state is a bureaucracy that caters primarily to the wishes of the rich and powerful means that it can alienate low-status groups and increase violence among them. Informal settlement is the opposite, being highly localized but closer in status to the principals. These twin features make it less repressive toward, and more popular with, disputants.

In light of the fragmentary nature of the available information on violence in state and, especially, stateless societies, all conclusions are necessarily tentative. My argument derives from a theoretical proposition that clearly requires further investigation and testing. Assuming that it is broadly correct, however, it implies that from the point of view of reducing violence, the optimal social system would combine the moderate status superiority of informal settlement with the extensive jurisdiction of the state.

# 4

# Configurations of War and Peace

Me and some friends were sitting around getting high. A friend of ours, Cal and his girlfriend, Janet came over and they told us that Cal had got stabbed in a fight by a guy called Charles. They asked us to go down there and help Cal.

We drove down. There were about four or five cars of us. Cal told us to bring our guns if we had them because they got guns down there. I had a .22 pistol which I picked up from our house. Some other guys did the same.

When we got there, they wasn't at where we thought they'd be at. So Cal drove us to a house. When we got out, he knocked at the door. A female and a guy I knew to see named Mikey came out. She said, "Charles ain't here." We got to arguing with Mikey, and my brother hit him on the head with a baseball bat. They pulled Mikey into the house and shut the door. We started to walk back to the cars. But one guy stopped and shouted, "Fuck this bullshit. I came to kill myself a nigger."[1] He went back and started kicking the door in. When it opened, we all went inside.

What occurred next is unclear. The narrator, Paul, claimed that after they were all inside the house his brother bumped into his arm, setting off the gun he was holding and causing him to kill Mikey accidentally. Whether it happened like that or not, Paul concedes that he shot the victim.

Perhaps the central feature of this case was that after Charles stabbed Cal, third parties joined in on both sides, creating a collective struggle. The partisanship (i.e., taking sides) of the third parties changed the conflict in several ways: it intensified the dispute (making it a group rather than just an individual affair), increased its scale (drawing in more people who could be injured or killed), and made alternative resolutions (such as avoidance) less likely.

Anybody can be a partisan—siblings, spouses, parents, children, friends, neighbors, acquaintances, or even total strangers. But under some conditions these same people will remain neutral or nonpartisan and become a force for peace, either by refusing to get drawn into the dispute or by seeking to settle it. A New York case illustrates how informal third-party ties can enhance peaceful resolutions of conflict:

> A dispute arose between the staff of a community center and some local men in their early 20s over the use of the center's basketball gymnasium. After the staff called the police to evict the men from the gymnasium, the men threatened to kill two staff members. The threats were not idle: the men were no strangers to violence and all had guns or access to them. However, violence was averted by the intervention of another member of the staff, Jackie, a young man who knew the members of the belligerent group. Jackie approached the group and persuaded the men not to shoot anyone but to come and discuss the problem with the head of the community center instead.
> (Described in Canada, 1995: 117–120)

In the former case, a group of friends adopted a partisan role, fomenting the conflict, escalating it to the point where a homicide occurred. In the latter, personal ties resulted in nonpartisan behavior, as Jackie engineered a peaceful resolution to a conflict that could well have resulted in one or more deaths. Between them, the two cases illustrate that the ties third parties have to others can be a source of violence or of peace depending on how they are configured in particular cases. A theory of partisanship developed by Black (1993b: chap. 7) allows us to specify which configurations of third-party ties will promote violence and which will facilitate peace.[2]

## Black's Theory of Partisanship

The purpose of Black's theory of partisanship is to predict when third parties will intervene to support others, how much support they will give, and the effect their support will have on the course the conflict takes. Black's theory explains a large body of findings from modern and premodern societies alike. Modified and extended, it explains even more.

### Relational Distance

Partisanship is a matter of degree, measurable by the amount of support a third-party provides and the personal costs and risks the support entails (Black and Baumgartner, 1983: 98). Treating partisanship as a form of "social gravitation" by which one person is attracted to another, Black (1993b: 126) proposes that "partisanship is a joint function of social closeness to one side and social distance from the other."

For these purposes, "social distance" has two dimensions: relational and cultural (Black, 1993b: 126). Relational distance, or intimacy, is the "degree to which people participate in one another's life" and can be measured by "the scope, frequency, and length of interaction between people, the age of their relationship, and the nature and number of links between them in a social network" (Black, 1976: 40–41).

Although people have a tendency to side with their intimates, they do not always do so. They can remain neutral, as, for example, a child might when its parents quarrel. In Black's theory what predicts partisan behavior is the intimacy of the third party's ties to *both* sides. ("Sides" include the principals and third parties; to simplify description of the theory I will refer only to third party–principal ties.) Partisanship intensifies with the inequality of third-party intimacy, with the degree to which the third party is relationally close or intimate with one principal and distant from the other. Conversely, partisanship weakens as third parties become equally intimate or distant from both principals. Figure 4-1 illustrates the theory:

P1                                                           P2

Tp1Tp1                        Tp3Tp3                        Tp2Tp2

Tp4Tp4

*Fig. 4-1.* Relational Closeness and Distance of Third-Party Ties.
KEY: P1, P2 = Principals; Tp = Third Party; White space = Relational Distance.

In figure 4-1, people in the position of Tp1 are close to one principal (P1) and distant from the other (P2) and are likely to be strongly partisan toward P1. Likewise, all Tp2s are likely to be strongly partisan toward P2. As the difference in closeness declines, third parties become less partisan. Third parties who are equally close or equally distant from both principals (Tp3 and Tp4) are expected to be neutral or nonpartisan. Equally close third parties (Tp3) will tend to engage in "warm nonpartisanship" by seeking an end to the hostilities. However, third parties who are equally distant from both principals (Tp4) are prone to be aloof and indifferent to the fate of the principals, to exhibit "cold nonpartisanship." (Black, 1993b: chap. 7)[3]

Black (1993b: 131–137) further argues that different partisan structures result in different types of conflict behavior. Thus, strong partisanship, on both sides, tends to result in sustained and reciprocal conflict. Tribal feuding and gang warfare are examples. As partisanship weakens, so too does the intensity of disputing. Warm nonpartisanship results in peacemaking, and cold nonpartisanship tends to elicit minimalistic conflict.

Black's theory of partisanship therefore yields the following proposition about third-party behavior:

*Violence increases with the relational closeness of third-party ties to one side and their distance from the other.*

The second component of social distance specified by Black is cultural distance, or the degree to which people are separated by differences of a symbolic nature, such as ethnicity, religion, or language. Black (1993b: 126) contends that cultural distance has the same effect on partisanship and conflict as relational distance. Thus, people are more likely to support a member of their own culture than a member of a different culture.

Since most interpersonal violence tends to take place within rather than across cultural groups, we have little information on the effect of cultural distance. However, a third type of social distance is clearly important in partisanship and violent conflict: organizational distance.

### Organizational Distance

Some partisans act as lone individuals, others act as members of groups to which one or both of the principals belong. Thus, partisans may be more or less distant from the principals in organizational space (Black, 1976: 93).[4] Organizational distance is minimal when two people belong to the same group and maximal when people belong to different groups. (Between these extremes lie the situations when both are nonmembers and one is and one is not a member, respectively.)

Third-party organizational distance seems to predict partisan behavior. Even without a tie of intimacy, the fact that two people are both members of the same organization makes them more likely to support each other. For example, in prison, a gang member is likely to align with those who belong to the same gang or gang alliance as he himself does, though he has little or no prior personal knowledge of them (Shakur, 1993). But as with relational distance, what best predicts partisanship and conflict is the third party's organizational closeness to and distance from both principals. Partisanship and enmities are most intense across organizational boundaries, between members of different groups. The most severe and sustained violent conflict consequently occurs between organized groups, such as modern gangs, and premodern lineages, clans, and villages.

Assuming that organizational distance has the same effect as relational distance, we can predict that when third parties are organizationally close to one of the principals (i.e., are members of the same organization) and organizationally distant from the other (i.e., are members of different organizations), they will give strong support. Third parties who are equally close organizationally (i.e., are members of an organization to which both principals belong) are likely to be warmly nonpartisan in trying to resolve the conflict. Third parties who belong to a different organization than the organizations belonged to by both principals, and, especially, third parties who belong to no organization at all, can be expected to remain aloof, to be coldly nonpartisan.

Existing theory suggests that the presence of organized partisans increases the likelihood of reciprocal violence (Black, 1993a: 75–78; 1995: 855 n. 130). So does empirical evidence. Consider, for example, prison gangs. The emergence of gangs in many American prisons in the 1970s and 1980s represents something of a natural experiment on the effects of organized groups because other factors that might have affected the amount of violence remained relatively constant. Thus, the same kind of people—the poor, marginal, unconventional, deviant, and minorities—were locked up in the prisons throughout the period. Despite this, prisons experienced a rapid increase in violence, including homicide (see, e.g., Jacobs, 1977: chap. 6; Irwin, 1980: 186–206; Porter, 1982; Ekland-Olson, 1986). In Texas, for instance, once "gangs, largely organized along racial lines," practicing "a feudlike system of justice" emerged in the prison system, the number of homicides increased eleven-fold in just a few years (from four in 1976–1978 to forty-six in 1982–1984) (Ekland-Olson, 1986: 398, 413). Gang members probably never constituted more than 3 percent of the Texas inmate population, yet they were "clearly implicated" in more than 60 percent (and suspected of involvement in another 10 percent) of the fifty-two prison homicides committed during 1984–1985 (calculated from Ekland-Olson, 1986: 412, including n. 7).

Note, however, that not all organized groups are prone to violence. Modern business corporations and religious organizations, for example, rarely, if ever, engage in violent conflict. Organizations clearly superior or inferior in status to third-party settlement agents are the most likely to pursue conflict violently. Hence, the present discussion should be read in conjunction with that in the previous two chapters.

Given that qualification, there appears to be a general principle:

*Violence increases with the organizational closeness and distance of third-party ties.*

## Configurations

Two dimensions of third-party ties, then, are especially important in explaining the course conflict takes: relational and organizational distance. Both are matters of degree. Together, they produce a large number of empirical combinations. In practice, however, some combinations appear more often and have greater impact on violence than others. Hence, the following discussion concentrates on several common combinations or configurations with a view to illustrating the powerful effect third-party ties have on conflict. The closer actual conflicts approximate these configurations, the more likely they should be to produce the associated effects.

### *Feuding without End: Close and Distant Group Ties*

The first configuration—close and distant groups—arises when third parties are connected by group and intimate ties to one principal and separated by group boundaries and distant ties from the other. If both sets of third parties have these characteristics, the result is two opposing groups of organized intimates who are strangers to one another (figure 4-2; note that a solid line indicates an organization).

*Fig.* 4-2. Close and Distant Group Ties

Black's amended theory of partisanship predicts that close and distant group ties will elicit the strongest partisan behavior as the third parties on each side commit wholeheartedly to the cause of their principal. The theory further predicts that conflicts with this configuration are apt to be protracted, reciprocal, and often lethal regardless of whether they occur in a remote tribal village or on the streets of a modern metropolis (see also Black, 1993a: 75–78; 1995: 855 n. 130). Evidence suggests that the theory is largely correct. Consider street gangs first.

### Street Warriors

We can define street gangs as age-graded groups that have at least minimal organization, some permanence, and distinctive symbolic representations of membership, and are not formed with the primary purpose of furthering conventional (e.g., sporting, artistic, educational) goals.[5] Gangs are often viewed by the public and academics alike as packs of lawless youngsters running wild, inflicting mayhem on one another, innocent bystanders, and entire neighborhoods without regard for life or property. Gangs, from this perspective, are degenerate, depraved, and disorderly.

A closer look reveals, however, that gangs are not chaotic groups beyond all moral boundaries. In fact, gangs inhabit a highly moral universe where issues of right and wrong with far-reaching consequences are often at the forefront of everyday life. The morality of gangs is, to be sure, different from that found in other sectors of modern society. For one thing, it is an older morality grounded in warrior values such as loyalty, honor, and vengeance. Moreover, it is a contentious rather than a harmonious morality. Gangs are prone to quarrel, struggle, and fight. Conflict is at the very heart of their existence.

Much gang conflict arises from disputes about territory. Thus, Frederic Thrasher's (1927: 6) colorful description of Chicago street gangs is as true today as when it was written in the 1920s.

> The hang-out of the gang is its castle and the center of a feudal estate which it guards most jealously. Gang leaders hold sway like barons of old, watchful of invaders and ready to swoop down upon the lands of rivals and carry off booty or to inflict punishment upon their enemies.

Regardless of whether it concerns territory, respect, protection of loved ones, or some other issue, conflict between gangs has several features more typical of warrior societies. One is that gang conflict is not just violent but feudlike as each side reciprocates in a tit-for-tat fashion for the injuries done to its members. A shooting of a gang member will commonly evoke a payback shooting, which, in turn, will evoke a payback, payback shooting, and so on until peace is made or the groups disintegrate. A second is that gang conflict typically exhibits collective liability under which any member of the gang (sometimes together with whatever bystanders happen to be present at the time) can be held responsible for the injury caused by one of the members (see, e.g., Black, 1983). In gang homicides, the killer is therefore less likely to have had prior contact with the victim and more likely to injure additional people than in nongang homicides (Klein, 1995: 115).

Both the reciprocal nature of gang feuding and collective liability are illustrated by the following case from Los Angeles in which a leading member of a gang was shot by a rival set. The following night his brother and six others stole a van, and armed themselves with an array of powerful guns. The shooting victim's brother recalls what happened next:

> "We drove from Second Avenue to Eleventh Avenue—most of the enemy was inside their houses. They knew there was gonna be retaliation, but, like idiots, some of 'em were out that night and we caught 'em. And we murdered 'em. . . . There was a party goin' on. We pulled the van up to the end of the street, got out real slow, careful not to talk or make a sound, and we slipped up on 'em. Then we started shooting. Everybody who was standin' in front of the house got hit. I remember there was one girl, she had on a black bomber jacket with white fur on the collar. She was the first to get hit, and I remember that fur just goin' red—bam—just like that. Looked like red flowers comin' out all over the white."
>
> (Quoted in Bing, 1991: 252–253)

Just how much homicide gangs commit is not easy to determine (Maxson and Klein, 1990). But inherent bellicosity, coupled with collective liability, ensures that gangs generate more than their fair share of assaults, lethal and otherwise (see, e.g., Moore et al., 1978: chap. 3; Horowitz, 1983: chap. 5; Vigil, 1988: 129–137; Klein and Maxson, 1989: 218; Toy, 1992; Sanders, 1994). Biographies of gang members, for example, emphasize the continual state of gang feuding (Bing, 1991; Shakur, 1993). But because those accounts naturally focus on the dramatic and memorable aspects of gang membership, it is hard to gauge from them just how deadly gang life actually is. Fortunately, a recent field study sheds some light on the matter.

For the study, a research team interviewed, over a period of two and one-half years, ninety-nine gang members active in the city of St. Louis. A small sample from a single setting like this is not representative of all gang members in the country. Moreover, violence among gang members fluctuates considerably in amount over time. Nonetheless, in the absence of more complete information, the results are clearly worth attending to. Five years after the interviews began, eleven of the ninety-nine gang members interviewed had been killed. For the interview group, then, the annual homicide rate per 100,000 for the five-year period was 2,222—some 230 times higher than the national rate (Decker and Van Winkle, 1996: 173). Or, to put the point slightly differently, during the study period a member of this group of St. Louis gang members was more than *two thousand times* more likely to be killed than the average citizen of countries such as England, Japan, France, or Singapore (see Reiss and Roth, 1993: 52).

## Gang Ties

What makes gang conflict so violent? Is it guns? Gangs today possess plenty of weapons, some highly sophisticated (see, e.g., Hagedorn, 1988: 143–144; Decker and Van Winkle, 1996: 175–176). Guns make it easier for gang members to kill people at long range; few people die from drive-by stabbings. On the other hand, the fact that everybody knows gangs have plenty of guns can also deter others from launching an attack against them. Overall, these effects may cancel each other out (Kleck, 1991). Even if they do not, and guns enhance the lethality of gang conflict, there are reasons why gangs arm themselves with guns in the first place. People whose lives are safe do not engage in an arms race. Weapons flourish where there already is violence (see, e.g., Horowitz, 1983; Sheley and Wright, 1995). Guns, and indeed weapons generally, are part of what needs to be explained.

Much the same is true of drugs, including alcohol. Gang members probably ingest more drugs and imbibe more alcohol than many of their peers (see, e.g., Hagedorn, 1988: 141–142; Decker and Van Winkle, 1996: 134–139, but see Sheley and Wright, 1995: chap. 5). But that alone cannot explain their violence. College students too have long been heavy drinkers and consumers of illegal drugs without being given to lethal conflict.

If drugs and alcohol fuel violence among gang members, it is only because gang members are already predisposed to violence. Once again, the task is to locate the social foundations of gang violence.

Central to gang violence is the structure of third-party ties, their closeness and distance, relational as well as organizational. Consider the relational element first. Most gang membership grows out of, and builds on, preexisting neighborhood friendships. Thrasher (1927: 28, 30) observed that "the majority of gangs develop from the spontaneous play-group" and that "the gang has its beginning in acquaintanceship and intimate relations which have already developed on the basis of common interests." Once gangs begin to form, members typically interact with one another intensively. Gang members spend a lot of time simply "hanging out" together. They watch television, go to movies, drink beer, smoke marijuana, play sports, cruise in automobiles, shop, look for members of the opposite sex, and the like (Decker and Van Winkle, 1996: 119). Belonging to a gang is not always a harmonious experience; members may have rivalries, tensions, and even fights among themselves (Horowitz, 1983: 100–101). But the many hours they spend together helps to build the intimacy on which gang partisanship thrives. Lengthy interaction simultaneously promotes relational distance from others by reducing members' involvement with people and groups outside the gang. In the St. Louis study, three-quarters of those who had been involved in legal groups (e.g., churches) dropped out after joining the gang (Decker and Van Winkle, 1996: 142).

Gangs are, in addition, groups with an identity (e.g., a name) and organizational structure (e.g., designated leaders, regular meetings) of their own. Gangs largely define themselves in opposition to one another. They maintain strong boundaries, with clear divisions between members and nonmembers, insiders and outsiders, friends and enemies. Their solidarity is typically reflected in and reinforced by a variety of symbols: "distinctive handshakes, hairstyles, stances, walks, battle scars, turf wars, hand signals, language, and nicknames" (Majors and Billson, 1992: 51). Their central demand is that members provide partisan support. Being organized, gangs exert a strong hold on the individuals who compose them. One former member of a Los Angeles gang, for example, has spoken of the "strong gravitational pull" of the gang and compared membership to belonging to a religion (Shakur, 1993: 103, 70). Echoing the analogy to religion, two other students of gangs remark that "standing up for your friends and fellow members is almost a sacred duty" (Decker and Van Winkle, 1996: 180).

The flip side of loyalty is opposition. If gang partisanship is, ideally, automatic, so too is enmity. Members of rival gangs should be resisted, come what may. The rights and wrongs of their actions are irrelevant. As a Los Angeles gang member put it, "You gotta understand—enemy got to pay just for bein' alive" (quoted in Bing, 1991: 43).

Gangs, then, bring together camaraderie and loyalty to one's own group and rivalry and hostility to others. When these conditions combine strongly, it is little wonder that conflict becomes so lethal.

## Preindustrial Feuding

The cross-cultural literature contains even more concentrated examples of close and distant group ties. In preindustrial, especially agricultural, societies kinship is often extremely strong and highly organized. Ties of kinship dominate social existence, obligating people to support their relatives at all times (see, e.g., Daly and Wilson, 1982: 374–375). As with modern gangs, kin-based partisanship has a quasi-religious intensity. To cite just one example, the Lugbara of Uganda, hold that "one of the most sacred duties of kinship is support for a fellow kinsman in his troubles" (Middleton, 1965: 46).

As well as having strong ties within groups, agricultural societies often have strong divisions between them. Kinship identity tends to be clear, language differences and other cultural markers pronounced, and the long chains of economic interdependency that bind people together in industrial society absent. Sharp boundaries demarcate lineages, villages, clans, tribes, or other groups one from the other.

This combination of closeness and distance—organizational and relational—creates the perfect conditions for reciprocal violence or feuding. Closeness means that people rush to the support of one another so that conflicts between individuals are soon transformed into conflicts between groups. Distance means that committed warriors can inflict maximum misery on the other side, unhindered by the restraints that come from shared ties.

One scholar has written of the interminable, eternal nature of feuding (Black-Michaud, 1975). Whether that is strictly true or not, preindustrial feuds can and sometimes do endure across several generations (Boehm, 1984). Behind most feuds lie committed and determined third parties who are slow to bury the hatchet. When somebody is killed, the victims' relatives and friends nurse the grievance, keeping it alive into the next generation and beyond. In Albania, for example, if a boy's father was murdered, "the child's mother and the neighbors told him of the crime as he grew up and urged him, failing another avenger, not to rest till he had done his duty" (Hasluck, 1954: 220). Another farming people, the Swat Pukhtun of Pakistan, have a proverb: "A Pukhtun waits for a century to take revenge and says, 'I took it quickly'" (Lindholm, 1982: 76). This is no idle boast. In one case, "A man was killed in a fight in the early 1950s. . . . After nearly thirty years, the son of the murdered man killed his father's killer while the old man was lying, helpless and immobile, in a hospital bed. This act . . . was much praised by the Pukhtun men" (Lindholm, 1982: 76–77).

Apart from Albania and the Swat Pukhtun, there are many examples of feuding societies in the cross-cultural literature: the Jalé and Mae Enga of New Guinea (Koch, 1974; Meggitt, 1977); the Jívaro of South America (Harner, 1972); nineteenth-century southeastern Chinese (see, e.g., Freedman, 1958: 81–86,

136–138); the Ifugao, Tausug, and Ilongot of the Philippines (Barton, 1919, 1938; Kiefer, 1972; Rosaldo, 1980); and the highlanders of Montenegro (Boehm, 1984).[6]

Theories of Feuding

To explain why people feud, anthropologists have developed two complementary theories, each of which emphasizes one characteristic of close and distant group ties. The first, known as fraternal interest group theory, stresses the role of intimate partisans bound together in organized groups (Thoden van Velzen and van Wetering, 1960; Otterbein and Otterbein, 1965; see also Thoden van Velzen and van Wetering, 1987; compare Ericksen and Horton, 1992). Backed up by a considerable amount of cross-cultural evidence, the theory proposes that societies in which male relatives reside in the same community are more violent than those in which they are dispersed across different communities.[7] Related men who live in the same place can and do support one another in disputes with outsiders. They thus form a series of strong warrior groups who are quick to use violence in the pursuit of grievances and to reciprocate for acts of violence against their members (see also Otterbein, 1968; Ross, 1986; Black, 1993a).

The second theory emphasizes the discreteness of organized groups or the social distance between them. The British anthropologist E. L. Peters was a proponent of this view. Reflecting on the Bedouin of Cyrenaica, a group among whom he spent time, Peters (1975: xxxvi) pointed to the territorial, economic, symbolic, and marital discreteness of each Bedouin kinship group in promoting violent exchanges. When conflict erupts, "discreteness means it is possible to dispense with compromise: it is the basis for decisive action." By contrast, when different groups have ties that link them together, "the pursuit of feud will be thwarted."

Although valid, both theories are incomplete and work better together rather than separately (see, e.g., Ross, 1993: 35–47).

Fraternal interest group theory does not pay enough attention to the relationship between organized groups. Conversely, discreteness theory gives insufficient emphasis to the ties within groups. It is the combination of both factors that elicits the reciprocal homicide that defines the feud.

## Violence as a Cause of Close and Distant Group Ties

Not only do close and distant group ties attract violence but violence tends to create close and distant group ties. Violence has the effect of intensifying the very conditions that produce it, thereby making it difficult to control.

Consider street gangs. One of the principal reasons that people join and stay in gangs is to protect themselves from danger (Decker and Van Winkle, 1996: 64–66, 73–74). Belonging to a gang means that the member does not have to face the risk of injury or death alone. Hence, a common effect of gang violence is that more people seek refuge in gangs and existing gangs become more cohesive (see, e.g., Klein, 1971; Hagedorn, 1988). However, strong gangs are apt to engage in longer and more lethal conflict, thereby increasing the gang member's overall risk of injury or death. A circular, self-perpetuating process is set in motion. Violence brings together people who seek protection and intensifies their partisan solidarity, but partisan solidarity intensifies gang violence, eliminates many gang members, and increases the danger from which people seek refuge in the first place (Decker and Van Winkle, 1996). In short, violence breeds gangs and gangs breed violence.

If this argument is correct, then declines in levels of violence should reduce the closeness and distance, relational and organizational, that underlie group violence. Here some New Guinea evidence is instructive. The Mae Enga are a group of farmers in the New Guinea highlands. Before colonization, they experienced much violent conflict between kinship groups organized along territorial lines. In the 1940s the Australian government began to extend its jurisdiction over Enga territory. The government established courts for the settlement of disputes and was largely successful in eliminating interclan violence. By the time Mervyn Meggitt, an anthropologist, visited the Enga in 1955, large-scale fighting had ceased for several years. Meggitt (1977: 153–154) found that the peace had had perceptible impacts on Enga social ties, loosening the bonds of solidarity and broadening the range of personal networks. Instead of just living in protective isolation with their own kin, people started to travel more to other localities for business and pleasure. They also began to build their houses closer to the borders of neighboring groups. Men ceased living with other men in warrior houses and moved into smaller family dwellings. Thus, the coming of peace weakened the system of close and distant group ties that had facilitated the traditional system of feuding.

In the 1960s, however, fighting broke out once more among the Enga. With the violence came a strengthening of the old pattern of social ties. People started to travel out of their home territory less often and to relocate their houses away from border zones, and men moved back into single-sex residences (Meggitt, 1977: 163). Once more, people began to huddle together in close-knit, mutually hostile groups. The renewed violence revitalized the social ties fostering the violence.

## Homicide without Feuding: Close and Distant Individual Ties

The second configuration—close and distant individual ties—occurs when third parties (1) are individuals rather than members of organized groups but are nonetheless (2) more intimate with one principal than the other (figure 4-3).

P1                                        P2

TpTpTpTp                                  TpTpTpTp

*Fig. 4-3.* Close and Distant Individual Ties

Close and distant individual ties are associated with less ardent partisanship (Black, 1993b: 132–134). Third parties still pitch in and help, but their partisan support is usually not as extreme as when they are members of organized groups. This configuration is also associated with intermediate amounts of violent behavior: violence is not as frequent or protracted as under close and distant group ties, but neither is it as infrequent as under equal ties (see also Black, 1993a: 75–78). Several examples illustrate the effects of close and distant individual ties. The first comes from my Virginia study.

### Virginia Homicide

Gang homicide receives a great deal of publicity, but it is by no means typical. Los Angeles County has, at the time of writing, the greatest number of gangs in the United States, but even there less than one-half of the homicides are committed by gangs (Klein, 1995: 114–115). Moreover, not every young man in socially disadvantaged neighborhoods belongs to a gang. A common alternative is for friends and brothers to spend a lot of time together and form small tight-knit cliques that are not organizationally demarcated one from the other. Members expect partisan support from one another; when one of the clique gets into trouble the others are required to join in to help their buddy. Though weaker than that found among gangs, this system of partisan support still promotes violent confrontations. It was well described by several of the young men I interviewed as they served time in Virginia prisons for murder or manslaughter.

Paul and Mikey's case discussed at the beginning of this chapter provides one example because without the intervention of friends and comrades on both sides (none of whom were gang members), the conflict would not, in all probability, have escalated into a homicide in the first place. Nor is this case an anomaly. Of the forty-two intentional, conflict-based homicides admitted by the Virginia defendants, fifteen (i.e., about one in three) involved partisans. Of these, twelve were cases in which third parties engaged in physical violence on behalf of another person. In three other cases, third parties provided verbal support for those in conflict. In two of these, third-party onlookers encouraged the use of violence; in the other, the killer was verbally attacked by a group, one of whom he killed.

Some of these other homicides were similar to Paul and Mikey's case in that two groups of young men confronted and fought one another. But there were other situations as well: one woman, for instance, stabbed a man who had slapped her son. In three cases, men came to the defense of women. Thus, a boyfriend killed the man who had attempted to rape his girl-friend; two men kidnapped and killed a man who had beaten one of their former girlfriends; and a man was paid by his sister and her friend to kill the friend's boyfriend, who was persistently violent toward their children.

### The Curious Absence of Vengeance

The Virginia cases have two additional features of interest: (1) not a single one was itself a retaliatory killing for a prior homicide, and (2) nor were any themselves avenged with a killing. Seventeen of the seventy-five prisoners interviewed (23 percent) reported that some kind of threat on their lives had been made following the homicide, but none came under gun-fire or were in danger of losing their lives. Most of the threats issued against them or their families seem to have been made for the sake of appearances; the victim's male relatives went through the preliminary motions of exacting vengeance. Even where their threats were more meaningful and they took steps to kill the killer, the conflict did not persist for very long. The se-quel to the case described in chapter 1 (in which Paul's friend,

George, killed a man in a public park in a dispute over a stolen bicycle) provides a representative example:

> The day Billy died two car loads of guys rolled by my Mom's house. One of them got out and asked for me. My sister answered the door. When she said I wasn't there, the guy pulled back his coat and showed her a big gun. He told her he was Billy's brother and she was to tell me he was looking for me. The following night they came around again. When George and I heard about it, we got our hardware [i.e., guns] and went to their neighborhood looking for them. We didn't find them. That was the end of it.

This is not untypical: One of the prisoners interviewed, for example, had met his victim's brother when he went to prison, yet they had talked without serious disagreement. Likewise, another prisoner had spent time in the same prison with the man who killed his brother. He too took no action.

Why did these men not carry through their threats and exact vengeance? They certainly did not lack motivation; they were part of an honor culture that commends and confers prestige on those who retaliate violently (an issue discussed in the next chapter). Some of them lived in a city (Richmond) that at the time had one of the ten highest rates of homicide in the country (*Richmond Times-Dispatch*, July 22, 1990, 1). Many were well used to violence, having grown up and lived surrounded by it all their lives. One man, for instance—still only in his middle twenties—said that he had probably witnessed anywhere from "five to eight" homicides in his life. To survive in this environment, the men had to learn to become violent themselves. They accepted that the proper way of dealing with a homicide is for the victim's male supporters—his brothers or close friends—to kill the killer. They distrusted legal officials, considering them corrupt and cooperation with the legal system inappropriate, even wrong. They had, in short, all the motivation they needed to exact vengeance.

Nor did the men lack the means to kill. Many people in their communities carried guns or kept guns in their homes. Those who did not could easily obtain one. One of the men traded in stolen guns and stated that he never had any shortage of customers, even though most of his stock consisted of large-calibre weapons, such as .41s and .44s.

The answer to the riddle lies in third-party ties. Individual ties are not conducive to long-term, reciprocal conflict. The interviewees were agreed that there were no gangs in their communities. Instead, there was the looser system of alliances centered on friendship ties, described earlier. Individuals hung together in small cliques that, however tight, were not organized. The cliques had no distinct organizational symbols and no identity apart from that of their current members. As a result, they were fragile. However determined their members may have been to stand by one another, the disappearance of one or more of them—whether through residential migration, imprisonment, or death—undermined the clique's existence. The clique depended on the presence of the current members and without them commonly fell apart. In sum, these individual close and distant ties resulted in partisanship that was strong enough to trigger initial acts of homicide but not strong enough to elicit retaliatory killings.

### Truncated Vengeance

What is true of modern societies is also true of tribal societies. Virtually all preindustrial people have strong ties of intimacy, but not all have organized kinship groups. My cross-cultural study shows that homicides in which the principals are not members of organized support groups are less likely to generate a vengeance homicide than those in which they are members. Table 4-1 divides the response to homicide into cases in which vengeance is typically exacted and those in which something short of vengeance (e.g., banishment, compensation) is the norm. Organized third-party ties are either present or absent.

TABLE 4.1.
*Vengeance as a Response to Homicide in Selected*
*Preindustrial Societies, by Presence of Organized*
*Third-Party Ties*

|  | Organized Third-Party Ties | |
|  | Absent (%) | Present (%) |
| --- | --- | --- |
| Vengeance | 10 | 81 |
| No vengeance | 90 | 19 |
| N | [20] | [16] |

NOTE: Chi square = 18.56; p < .001.

The effect of organized supporters evident in table 4-1 can
also be seen by comparing types of tribal society. In general, kinship organization is not as central to hunter-gatherers as it is to
agricultural people. Thus, one anthropologist has written that a
"relative lack of sustained reciprocal load-bearing relationships
is widely characteristic of the social organization of nomadic
hunter-gatherers" (Woodburn, 1979: 258). He illustrates his argument by reference to the Hadza of Tanzania, who, he says,
"have to solve their disputes for themselves almost always without any intervention by third parties." This arrangement means
that "the great majority of disputes do not . . . lead to violence . . .
[but] are resolved by self-segregation" (Woodburn, 1979: 252).
Even so, occasional homicides do occur. When they do, "the kin
of the victim can expect no compensation and are themselves unlikely to retaliate against the murderer," who typically moves
away from the victim's kin (Woodburn, 1979: 252).

Hunter-gatherers, then, typically do not have the same pronounced kinship divisions that so often characterize agricultur-
alists. They also have less feuding (Daly and Wilson, 1988:
224; Ericksen and Horton, 1992). Consider, for example, two
of the most-studied hunter-gatherer groups: the Ju/'hoansi and
the Eskimos. Both groups have some homicide: people kill to
eliminate incorrigible deviants, in the course of fights, as a result of adultery or seeking revenge. But they rarely, if ever, have
long feuds: if killings are avenged, the vengeance is not usually

itself avenged (Lee, 1979: 382–400; Balikci, 1970: 179–185, 189–192).[8]

There is an exception, but it is one that supports the point being made (e.g., Woodburn, 1979: 258–260). Australian Aborigine groups such as the Murngin (Warner, 1958) and the Tiwi (Hart and Pilling, 1979) feud extensively and consequently have high rates of homicide. Thus, the Murngin had, over a twenty-year period, a homicide rate more than ten times higher than that of the Ju/'hoansi, the only other hunter-gatherer people for whom a homicide rate has been calculated (330 compared to 29 per 100,000) (Warner, 1958: 157, 158–159; Lee, 1979: 397–398).[9] But the Murngin have ties that are considerably more organized than those of the Ju/'hoansi and most hunter-gatherers. In fact, they have a series of ties to relatives in other organized kin groups that obligate them to provide partisan support and that tend to escalate conflict:

> The kinship system of the Murngin, with its attendant set of obligations, duties, rights and privileges . . . tends to enlarge the scope of a two-clan feud to four or possibly all of the clans of the several tribes. The *waku-gawel* relationship, and also the *dué-galle, mari-kutara,* and *marelker-gurrong* relationships express a very strong solidarity; and a man can depend on any one of these relatives, distributed in eight or more clans besides his own, to come to his assistance. An isolated killing, owing to the strength of the kinship structure, usually results in the whole of northeastern Arnhem Land becoming a battle ground at fairly frequent intervals.      Warner (1958: 156)

In short, the Murngin and several other Aboriginal cultures are unusual among hunter-gatherers in having strong, organized kinship groups, and that helps to explain why they are unusually violent.

## The Dilemma of Violence: Cross-Cutting Ties

In the third configuration, third-party organizational distance and relational distance cross-cut each other. This can happen in several ways. One common form of cross-cutting ties occurs when third parties are relationally close to but organizationally distant from one principal and relationally distant from but organizationally close to the other principal (figure 4-4).

*Fig. 4-4.* Cross-Cutting Ties

Cross-cutting ties create a dilemma for third parties: if they support one side, they will jeopardize their relationship with the other side. At the same time, their close ties make it hard for them to stay out of the conflict altogether. Many third parties respond by engaging in the informal settlement described in the previous chapter, becoming what Black (1993b: 135) calls a warm nonpartisan. For this reason, cross-cutting ties tend to inhibit violence and to promote peaceful outcomes to conflict. The cross-cultural literature provides many examples.

## The Power of Cross-Cutting Ties

The first person to emphasize the power of cross-cutting ties was an anthropologist, Elizabeth Colson (1953), in a well-known paper she wrote on the Plateau Tonga, a farming people of southern Zambia. Colson was interested in how the Tonga could live so peaceably in the absence of any government. Her answer was that Tonga society is made up of dense, cross-cutting ties that encourage people to resolve their conflicts peacefully. When disputes arise, the principals receive support from their mothers' and fathers' kinship groups, as traced through matrilineal descent, the mother's line. But some members of those groups will typically have close ties to the other side. This is because Tonga kinship groups are not concentrated in one locality but dispersed across many different settlements. People develop close relationships with their neighbors, regardless of whether they are kin or not, because neighbors cooperate in farming, herding, and the performance of community rituals. Overall, Tonga society is characterized by a complex web of crisscrossing ties based on family, residence, religion, friendship, and work. It is a rare conflict, therefore, in which there are no third parties caught in the middle with connections to both sides to act as peacemakers. The net result is a high degree of peace and order, despite the absence of the state.

There are several ways in which cross-cutting ties can serve to reduce violence. People who find themselves in the middle of conflicts may try to persuade the principals and their supporters to talk instead of fight. Similarly, they might seek to mediate the conflict. Alternatively, they sometimes simply separate the disputants, physically restraining them from attacking one another, a tactic found among groups as diverse as Turkish villagers (Stirling, 1965: 248–249); the Dou Donggo of Indonesia (Just, 1991: 304); sedentary Australian Aborigines (McNight, 1986: 146); Eskimos (van den Steenhoven, 1962: 76); the Tory islanders of Ireland (Fox, 1962); and the Nuer of Sudan (Evans-Pritchard, 1940: 151).

The cross-cutting ties argument enjoys a considerable amount of support (e.g., Gluckman, 1969: chap. 1; Murphy, 1957; Horwitz, 1990: 131–136; Senechal de la Roche, 1990: 141–151). Perhaps the most extensive evidence comes from a survey by Marc Howard Ross (1986, 1993) of ninety preindustrial societies. Ross found that societies with multiple reference groups (e.g., kinship, age, ritual) have less internal conflict—including violence—than societies in which people are organized around a single axis (compare Kang, 1976).

Ross's study analyzes societies, but the same holds true of individual conflicts. In my cross-cultural study, I analyzed the response to homicide within different relationships across societies. I divided partisan networks into two categories—discrete and cross-cutting—depending on whether the two sides' supporters had ties to each other or not. The results were clear-cut: when the third parties have discrete ties, four out of five (83 percent) homicides lead to a vengeance killing (i.e., any retaliatory killing); when their ties are cross-cutting, that proportion drops to two out of five (38 percent) (table 4-2). (Note that although the results do not attain conventional levels of statistical significance, they are based on a small sample.)

TABLE. 4.2.
*Vengeance as a Response to Homicide in Selected*
*Preindustrial Societies, by Cross-Cutting*
*Third-Party Ties*

|  | Third-Party Ties | |
|---|---|---|
|  | Cross-cutting (%) | Discrete (%) |
| Vengeance | 38 | 83 |
| No vengeance | 62 | 17 |
| N | [34] | [24] |

NOTE: Chi square = 4.70; p < .10.

## Illustrations

As further illustrations of the abstract cross-cutting ties effect displayed in table 4-2, consider several concrete examples. Take, for instance, the great contrast in violence between two societies discussed in the previous chapter: the Semai of Malaya and the Waorani of Ecuador.

Two anthropologists who earlier studied the Semai—Clayton and Carole Robarchek (1992)—became interested in Waorani violence because, on the surface at least, the two groups are very similar. Both live in remote equatorial rain forests and subsist through a combination of shifting, or swidden, agriculture and hunting. Both are organized into politically autonomous bands, typically with fewer than one hundred people. Both have bilateral kinship, are highly egalitarian, and have similarly indulgent patterns of child rearing. Yet the Semai are one of the most peaceful societies ever observed, and the

Waorani, by contrast, have one of the highest rates of homicide ever recorded.

Seeking to explain the differences in violence, the Robarcheks studied the Waorani at first hand for themselves. They found that economic scarcity—a factor cited by some theorists to explain violence within and between structurally simple societies—does not supply the answer; an adult Waorani has much more land and food available to him or her than a Semai. A more telling difference between the two groups lies in their social ties. Semai rely on their relatives or kindred to help them in times of sickness, need, and conflict. But kindreds overlap, with the result that in conflict the relatives of any two opposed individuals will likely include people who are related to both (1992: 202). The Waorani, however, rely on immediate family rather than kindred for help. Moreover, because the norm for them is to marry an offspring of a parent's different-sex siblings (e.g., a son marries a daughter of one of his father's sisters or mother's brothers; a daughter marries a son of one of her mother's brothers or father's sisters), the kindred is split into two groups: those classified as parents and siblings and those classified as potential spouses and in-laws and with whom disputes are frequent.[10] The result is that far from being characterized by dense interdependent ties that restrain the disputants, Waorani conflict typically pits two relationally independent groups against each other.

Cross-cutting ties explain variation in violence not only across societies but within them as well. Rural Mexico provides an example. For students of violence, Mexico is an especially interesting region of the globe because some, though not all, of its towns and villages have extremely high rates of killing (Friedrich, 1962; Nash, 1967; Schwartz, 1972; Romanucci-Ross, 1973; Greenberg, 1989). Anthropologist Laura Nader encountered this sharp variation within the small region of Oaxaca that she studied: in thirteen villages, the average annual homicide rate ranged, over a ten-year period (1953–1962), from 0 per 1,000 people to 10 per 1,000 (1990: 170).

In explaining these sharp differences, Nader found that the villages with high rates of homicide were split into discrete factions and those with low rates were knit together by multiple cross-linking ties. The seven factionalized villages had homicide rates ranging from 2 to 10 per 1,000. Of the six nonfactionalized villages, four had no homicide at all, and two had rates of 1 and 2 per 1,000, respectively.

The Mexican example compares different villages at the same time. A study from rural Pakistan provides an excellent demonstration of how the growth and decline of cross-cutting ties within a single community affects its rate of violence at different times. Located in the remote Hindu-Kush mountains, Thull is a community of about six thousand people. R. Lincoln Keiser, an anthropologist who worked there in the 1980s, was struck by the extremely high levels of violence: "One cannot live in Thull for even a day," he writes, "without becoming aware of the pervasiveness of organized violence"; residents possess an astonishing array of weaponry, and gunshots "are heard continually during the day and often times in the night as well. . . . Gunfire has become the music of Thull" (Keiser, 1986: 490). In recent years, "the number of murders and assaults has so increased that the local Pakistani police, well acquainted with violence in rural communities, simply shake their heads in resignation, stating that the people of Thull are among the worst, most lawless in Pakistan" (Keiser, 1986: 490).

Thull was not always violent; oddly enough, it became so only in the fifteen years or so since the community began to modernize. In the 1970s, schools, a hospital, and new roads were built, electricity and telephones were installed, and television became part of the culture. As these changes occurred, violence, including murder, increased dramatically.

One of the major reasons for the surge in violence, Keiser argues, was the decline in cross-cutting social ties within the community. Before modernization, the dominant economic activity in Thull was the herding of goats and cattle. Pastures were divided among groups, called *lud*, composed of men from the three lineages into which Thull clans are grouped.

> Thus people who herded together, who had common rights to pastures and common interest in protecting these rights, were often the very people who opposed one another in clan disputes. In this classic system of conflicting allegiances political interests and moral sentiments crosscut one another, as men opposed in certain contexts joined together in others. Settling disputes without violence not only upheld the value of village peace, but also allowed [people] to avoid painful political choices between *lud* and clan allies.
>
> (Keiser, 1986: 498)

Economic modernization changed all of this. After roads were built, growing potatoes for external sale replaced herding as the primary economic activity. Since potato farming requires less cooperation than herding, the number of cross-cutting ties in the community declined sharply. People became less dependent on their neighbors. As that happened, the old restraints no longer operated, and violence became an increasingly attractive way of settling disputes.

## Cross-Cutting Ties Today

In modern societies, the demise of strong kinship groups means that cross-cutting ties are no longer as common as they once were. Nevertheless, the gang literature contains several, albeit unsystematic, illustrations of the power of cross-cutting ties. Two incidents recounted in the autobiography of a former Los Angeles gang member, for instance, provide examples of how ties of intimacy that cross-cut organizational ties can reduce violence even among the most hardened of street warriors. The first:

> Two gangs, the Eight Trays and Hoovers, had supported one another in previous wars with other gangs. But when the Hoovers became involved in a war with the East Coast, the Eight Trays remained neutral because some of the people in their neighborhood had relatives in both the Hoovers and East Coasts. (Described in Shakur, 1993: 261–266)

The second incident:

> Two individuals, Monster and Lunatic Frank, had been friends for a long time but had joined rival gangs. One night as Monster was accompanying his girlfriend to her home he was surrounded by a group that included Lunatic Frank. Monster was unarmed, but Lunatic Frank dissuaded his companions from killing Monster and his girlfriend.
>
> Three weeks later, one of Monster's fellow gang members, Tray Stone, captured Lunatic Frank, marching him back to Tray Stone's territory at gun point. This time, Monster insisted that Lunatic Frank be released unharmed, much to Tray Stone's chagrin.
>
> (Described in Shakur, 1993: 345–347)

Unfortunately, it is impossible to assess how representative these incidents are. No data exist that would permit a reliable calculation of how often cross-cutting ties serve to dampen conflict. But the highly individual nature of the ties found in many sectors of modern society suggest that organizational and relational ties now cross-cut much less often than they once did. This would explain why so many homicides today involve third parties who observe the principals fighting but do not intervene to stop them. In a well-known study, David Luckenbill (1977) analyzed seventy conflicts that ended in homicide in a California county. He found that in thirty-two there had been a previous violent encounter between the parties, and in about half of these a third party had intervened to make peace (1977: 184 n. 3). But he also found that seven out of ten homicides were committed before third-party witnesses. In more than half (57 percent) of these, the third parties encouraged one or both principals to engage in violence; in the remaining cases (43 percent), they remained aloof. These latter two scenarios suggest that distant third-party ties, and with them cooler forms of nonpartisanship, may be more prevalent under modern conditions.[11]

## Organizational and Relational Closeness

Before turning to analyze distant third-party ties, it might be noted that cross-cutting ties do not invariably and automatically prevent an outbreak of violence (e.g., Hallpike, 1977: vi, 229; Knauft, 1990: 276–278; table 3-2, above). Cross-cutting ties often mitigate conflict without actually preventing two groups from fighting. In some societies, people with ties to both sides are excused from participating in vengeance raids, though the raids go ahead anyway (Chagnon, 1988: 988). In others, individuals with cross-cutting ties are sometimes allowed to avoid killing one another even as they participate on opposing sides in a fight (see, e.g., Lewis, 1961: 140). In both instances, the cross-cutting ties create a kind of private peace treaty, limited to a few people, in the midst of a larger war. These ties do not noticeably reduce the overall amount of lethal violence, but they do decrease the probability that particular people will kill particular others.

Cross-cutting ties reduce violence because they reduce third-party social distance. The closer third parties are to both principals, the more likely the conflict is to attract a peaceful resolution (Black, 1993b: chap. 7). Thus, the more a conflict takes on the shape shown in figure 4-5, the greater the probability that it will be resolved peacefully.

*Fig. 4-5.* Close Ties

My cross-cultural study provides some empirical support. In the societies I sampled, the homicides least likely to generate vengeance homicide were those in which the killing involved intimate members of the same organization. Table 4-3 compares cases in which the killing took place within or between kinship groups who occupy their own territories, thus ensuring that third parties will be relationally as well as organizationally close to—or distant from—the principals. The table presents a rare example of a perfect association.

TABLE 4.3.
*Vengeance as a Response to Homicide in Selected Preindustrial Societies, by Organizational and Relational Distance of Third-Party Ties*

| | Organizational and Relational Third-Party Ties | |
| --- | --- | --- |
| | Close (%) | Distant (%) |
| Vengeance | 0 | 100 |
| No vengeance | 100 | 0 |
| N | [16] | [16] |

NOTE: Chi-square = 32.00; p < .000001.

A point worth noting is that the lack of vengeance following homicides between intimate members of the same group is not because the killing generates no anger or condemnation. In fact, in many preindustrial societies, the worst thing somebody can do is to kill a close relative. Among the Lugbara of Uganda, for example, a man who kills a member of his own lineage commits "a sin for which there is no humanly awarded punishment. . . . People . . . fear and avoid him as unnatural" (Middleton, 1965: 51). Despite their abhorrence of his action, the Lugbara do not kill the killer; the combination of group unity and intimacy puts the victim's closest supporters too close to the killer to exact vengeance. This is true of many tribal societies. As E. L. Peters observed of the Bedouin of Cyrenaica: "The notion of corporate identity is so strong that it eliminates the use of penal action against one of its members for the greatest offense of all" (Peters, 1967: 264).

Third-party closeness, then, is a matter of degree. Cross-cutting ties represent an intermediate degree of closeness. As such, they mitigate conflict and render lethal vengeance less likely. But cross-cutting ties do not guarantee peace. When third parties are simultaneously relationally and organizationally close to both principals, the probability of nonviolent resolutions of conflict becomes ever more likely.

## Peaceful Indifference: Distant Individual Ties

Distant individual ties, the final configuration, consists of third parties who are (1) equally distant from both principals and (2) individuals rather than members of organized groups (figure 4-6).

Pᵢ                    P2

Tp

*Fig. 4-6.* Distant Individual Ties

Distant individual ties is a highly individualistic configuration in that the principals are typically left to handle conflict on their own. Third parties who are not members of organizations and have no prior relationship with the principals are usually slow to intervene at all, exemplifying Black's (1993b: 134) principle of "cold nonpartisanhip." As Black notes, this arrangement appears, on the whole, to promote the use of nonviolent outcomes to conflict, although there are also some important exceptions.

### Modernization

The experience of Europe over the past six centuries or so demonstrates how more distant third-party ties tend to reduce violence. Most European countries today enjoy extremely low rates of homicide; they did not always. In earlier times, Europeans were a bloody lot, much given to violent conflict (Elias, [1939] 1978: 191–205). In the thirteenth century, for example, England had a homicide rate that was at least ten times higher than it is today (Gurr, 1981; see also Stone, 1983). Norwegian rates have declined tenfold since the middle of the sixteenth century (Næshagen, 1995). And homicide in Holland and Sweden shows similar reductions since the fifteenth century (Spierenburg, 1996; Österberg, 1996).

A major social trend of this kind is almost certainly the result of several factors. One that seems central is the individualization of conflict. "One of the most striking features of medieval homicide [was] its markedly collective character" writes James Given (1977: 41) in his study of thirteenth-century English homicide. Given found that more than six out of ten people accused of homicide at that time killed with a named companion. Though comparable modern English data are not available, only about one in ten homicides known to United States police in the years 1980–1984 involved multiple offenders and/or victims (Williams and Flewelling, 1988: 425). Even if these figures underestimate the involvement of partisans in modern homicide, there is little doubt that homicide is considerably more individuated today than it was in England six hundred years ago. Then it was an affair of groups; now it often involves individuals only.[12]

The highly collective nature of medieval and early modern homicide is unsurprising in light of the strong social ties that characterized pre-modern societies:

> Medieval men and women lived not only their economic but their personal lives in the company of, and under the eye of, other people. Individualism was not prized in the abstract, and privacy was rare in practice. Peasants lived in crowded one-room cottages, working, eating, and making love elbow to elbow with family and, on really cold nights, livestock. Even the greatest houses lacked many truly private rooms, with doors and locks; owners, spouses, children, servants, visitors, retainers, and dogs continually jostled each other through the arches. Very little was done alone—including, it seems, murder.
>
> (Lane, 1997: 19–20)

Less partisanship helps to explain why, for example, aristocratic violence has declined so sharply over the centuries. Consider the English aristocracy (Stone, 1965: chap. 5). As we saw in the previous chapter, English aristocrats of the fifteenth and sixteenth centuries were no strangers to violent conflict. They invariably carried a weapon in public, and from time to time they had occasion to use it. Their violence was facilitated and fueled by the large body of men—lesser gentry, retainers, and servants—whom they attracted to their households. In the mid-fifteenth century, the earl of Northumberland, for example, had 171 people on his household staff; in the 1550s Lord Berkeley lived in London with 150 servants, all of whom wore his colors. The members of an aristocrat's retinue did not merely provide domestic service; they were expected to act as bodyguards and to fight for their lord when trouble arose. The result was frequent armed brawling between rival gangs of aristocrats.

Gradually, however, the size of aristocratic retinues shrank, with the result that by the mid-seventeenth century, the households of the elite were considerably smaller than they had been previously. Although aristocratic violence was not yet eliminated (dueling was still to reach its heyday), and although it was by no means the sole factor at work, the weakening of lord-follower bonds and the consequent reduction in the size of bands of armed retainers were factors that helped to wean the nobility from "their age-old habits of casual violence" (Stone, 1965: 269).

## Suburban Harmony

In modern societies, the distant ties that so often characterize social life create many occasions for third-party nonintervention or cold nonpartisanship. Cold nonpartisanship, in turn, helps to explain why many sectors of these societies experience relatively little violence.

Suburbs are a good example. The handling of conflict in a suburb is the subject of an ethnographic study conducted by M. P. Baumgartner (1988) in a town outside New York City. As expected, Baumgartner found that the town has low levels of violent conflict. Yet people have frequent interpersonal disagreements of the kind that in other settings often lead to violence: inconsiderate neighbors, rowdy teenagers, personal incompatibilities, and so forth. But these conflicts rarely lead to violent crime. People handle the great majority of their disputes nonconfrontationally. In most instances, residents prefer to tolerate the problem or avoid the offender. Rarely do they seek the advice of lawyers over their interpersonal problems and rarer still do they sue one another. If they mobilize the police, they typically do so anonymously. Overall, a distinctive social morality prevails, a morality that Baumgartner calls "moral minimalism," the characteristics of which are that most disputes have short life spans and remain matters of private concern, that people shun the use of aggressive tactics, and that social interaction is highly peaceable.

Suburbanites tend to be affluent, educated, and of high social status in general. While this helps to explain their low levels of violence, a more powerful factor is their distinctive social ties. Viewed in cross-cultural perspective, suburban ties are noteworthy for their weakness: relationships tend to be transient and restricted to a single dimension of interaction, networks are individualized and shifting, levels of privacy are high, and those of interdependency are low. As Baumgartner (1988: 128) summarizes it:

> People in the suburbs move in and out of relationships frequently and live their lives under conditions of privacy, individuation, material independence, and freedom from authority, all the while surrounded by a variety of competing interests and associates. This makes the avoidance of moral trouble feasible and attractive, and confrontation less so.

These loose, distant ties have the effect of reducing partisanship. When people are strangers or only distantly acquainted, they are normally slow to intervene in the conflicts of others. And "without supporters to help in the management of their conflicts, people are more likely to forego direct confrontations" (Baumgartner, 1988: 97). Moreover, the absence of partisan supporters means that any violence that does erupt is unlikely to spread.

The relationship between lack of third-party intervention and low levels of violence is borne out by the only systematic exception to the high degree of order found in the town. Baumgartner (1988: 97) reports that although the teenaged and working-class residents of the town are not especially violent by, say, inner-city standards, they do "engage in more aggressive and open conflict than middle-class adults." One feature that distinguishes these groups from the adult and middle-class inhabitants is that their ties are closer. They have longer and more intense relationships, their networks are more tightly woven, and their conflicts are, consequently, more collective. Disputes involving young people and working-class residents are more likely to attract partisan intervention. Partisan supporters will often pitch in to help their relatives and friends, with the result that the overall level of aggression tends to rise.

## Domestic Violence and Isolation

There are, however, several sets of circumstances in which distant individual third-party ties and cold nonpartisanship are associated with elevated levels of violent conflict. One example occurs when physical fights are already under way (Luckenbill, 1977; Felson, 1978, 1982). Here, the failure of third parties to restrain the principals can result in more violence not just because the principals are free to inflict injury but also because considerations of personal honor may dictate that they not back down in front of an audience. The next chapter explores the latter scenario.

Domestic conflict may provide a second example of how third-party nonintervention can escalate conflict. Domestic violence occurs most often in families that are socially isolated (Gelles, 1987: 132–137; Tucker and Ross, 1998; see also Baumgartner, 1993). Isolation means that outsiders are unlikely to learn of the violent behavior, and even if they do, are unlikely to do anything about it. Moreover, intimate aggressors will often take steps to resist intervention from the outside. For instance, if they have a quarrel with their intimate in public, they will usually turn violent only in the privacy of the dwelling ("Just you wait till we get home") (see, e.g., Gelles and Straus, 1988: 93). Privacy enables aggressors to go about their business free from external constraint while ensuring that their victims have nobody to defend them from further attacks. Without third parties, domestic violence can escalate on its own momentum.

When, then, will nonintervention increase violence and when will it dampen it? The answer awaits further investigation, but the intimacy and relational stability of the principal parties are, perhaps, important considerations. When the principals are intimates and relatively immobile, they cannot easily escape one another, and their conflict can easily intensify. Nonintervention by third parties may therefore increase violence. On the other hand, when the parties are not intimates and/or mobile, they can more readily avoid one another. Under these circumstances, third-party intervention may strengthen conflict, and nonintervention dissipate it.

## Settlement and Moralism

Another important qualification to the argument that distant ties promote peaceful resolutions of conflict relates to settlement agents. As we have seen, Black's theory predicts that third parties generally do not involve themselves in the conflicts of strangers, and the evidence is consistent with this. But sometimes they do intervene, for example, when it is their job to do so. Legal officials are the classic modern example of people who routinely find themselves called upon to settle disputes of total strangers.[13]

Relationally distant settlement agents, Black (1993b: chap. 8) argues, handle cases much like their vertically distant counterparts: in a detached and severe, or moralistic, fashion. Settlement agents who are strangers do not involve the principals much in the resolution, are not given to compromise, focus heavily on abstract rules rather than the equities of the particular case, and are often quite punitive and coercive (Black, 1993b: 145–149). As we saw previously, none of these traits endears them to disputants. Relationally distant settlement agents are therefore often not very popular; people steer clear of them if they can. Moreover, the more distant the settlement agent, the greater the rejection. Rejection therefore sets into motion the dynamic discussed earlier: disputants do not seek out the settlement agents and thereby become more likely to employ violent means of redressing grievances.

In the main, then, distant individual ties appear to promote nonviolent outcomes to conflict. But not always. Under some conditions—the nature of which is still not entirely clear—third-party strangers can promote violence.

To reiterate the argument: simple mathematical calculation tells us that, all other things being equal, conflict between groups will generate more injury and death than that between individuals: if one-half of the people involved in a conflict are injured or killed, there will be one injury or death when two people are involved and five deaths when ten people are. The highest rates of violence—in modern and premodern societies alike—are therefore generally found where groups of antagonists confront one another. To understand violence, then, it is important to understand the formation and effect of groups in conflict and to understand partisan behavior.

Black's theory of partisanship, altered to include organizational distance, allows us to predict when third parties will intervene as partisans and when their intervention will most likely lead to violence. Thus, the theory proposes that third parties lend strong partisan support under two main conditions: when they are intimate with and a member of the same organized group (e.g., gang, lineage) as is one principal, and relationally distant from and a member of a different organized group than is the other principal. The theory further proposes that third-party organization and relational distance combine to produce different kinds of conflict. Close and distant group ties make for prolonged and reciprocal lethal conflict. Close and distant individual ties result in individual acts of homicide. Cross-cutting ties encourage informal settlement, and the closer the third parties are to both principals, the less likely violence becomes. Distant individual ties for the most part elicit peace.

These conflict configurations by no means exhaust all the empirical possibilities. Many others can be found in practice, and in the future scholars will have to isolate and analyze them (e.g., where one party is and the other is not a member of an organized group). The configurations discussed in these pages, however, do represent some of the more commonly occurring ones.

# 5

# Foundations of Honor

We were both selling cocaine. Calvin was the big dealer in our neighborhood. He was only 17 but a good friend of mine. Everybody got their drugs from him. I didn't sell in the neighborhood but at a factory in town.

One day I gave a guy an 8-ball [i.e., an eighth of an ounce] and told him he could sell it provided he didn't tell anybody where it came from. But this guy told people and the word spread that I had very good coke [i.e., cocaine]. Seeing as everybody knew where it came from there didn't seem to be any point in holding it back any longer. So I started selling. Stood out on the street like all the others.

Soon most of Calvin's customers started coming to me. He cut his coke; I didn't.

One day Calvin and two of his henchmen confronted me. He said "I hear you been selling up there. If I was to come up there you couldn't sell shit." To me, he was disrespecting me. I said "Man, if you disrespect me again I won't be responsible for what I do to you." He got loud: "Who the fuck do you think you is?" I repeated what I said and walked away.

Next day, he come up on the dope stroll. I can't remember his exact words but he told me not to sell there. I said he didn't own it. He said "Don't be here when I come back." I waited for him all day but he didn't come.

That same day, two of my friends told me that they had just heard that Calvin had a contract out on me. They didn't know who was going to fill it but I had a pretty good idea.

That night, I went to a girl's house. I did coke all night. Didn't sleep at all. My two friends came around in the morning and we did more coke. It was a Saturday and I was

> throwing a block party. I had a DJ out on a back porch play-
> ing music. I bought cases of beer and gave people reefer [i.e.,
> marijuana].
>
> When I go outside there's a lot of people on the street, in-
> cluding Calvin. When I seen him I walked up to him. He was
> talking to a guy. I interrupted him. I said "Have you got a
> motherfuckin' problem with me?" He said "No. Have you
> got one with me?" I then said "You ain't shit, man." He
> swung and hit me with his fist. Then he reached for his waist
> band. I knew he kept his .357 there. I was quicker. I got my
> .38 out and shot him in the hand. The bullet went through
> his hand and hit him in the abdomen. He turned and started
> trotting away. I heard people saying to me "Don't do it.
> Don't do it." But I fired and hit him in the side of his back.
> He fell on the ground.

At one level, this case is just another dispute between
rival drug dealers. But to see it simply as an instance of the elimination of a business rival is to miss the underlying conflict over
pride, respect, or honor. Dividing the narrator, Peter, and Calvin
was not just a squabble over drug turf but a more fundamental
disagreement over personal honor. In this respect, the case is
typical of a great many homicides, in modern and premodern
societies alike.

## Classical Honor

Honor is a complex concept that means different things to different people (Stewart, 1994). Today, it often refers to honesty
or moral integrity. Somebody who invariably tells the truth or
who does the right thing even at personal cost is said to be honorable. In many societies, however, "honor" has a quite different meaning and connotes the status that attaches to physical

bravery: to be honorable is to be bold and valiant. Where honor in this sense is found so too is violent conflict because "the ultimate vindication of honor lies in physical violence" (Pitt-Rivers, 1966: 29).

Honor as bravery is part of a larger ethical system, a code of behavior. Admittedly, not everybody sees it that way. To those beyond its boundaries, a culture that esteems honor often appears as the antithesis of a moral community, governed by the law of the jungle, rewarding brute force over every other human attribute. Yet for those subject to it, honor is far from being a chaotic system of domination by the strong of the weak. On the contrary, the requirements of honor represent a moral way of life in which courage, independence, and a good reputation are central values. All honor cultures have clear rules of right and wrong, including, most centrally, when violence is and is not justified. Their core injunction is clear: Resist—with force, if necessary—any attempt to disrespect or dominate you. An honorable person therefore responds aggressively to insult, is willing to defend his or her property, and is sure to exact vengeance for certain kinds of offenses, such as the killing of a close relative.

## The Heart of Honor

Most societies probably contain some elements of honor, but honor plays a much more central role in some groups than others. People who strongly emphasize honor—honor societies or honor cultures—exist or have existed in all parts of the globe. They include the highlanders of Albania (Hasluck, 1954) and Montenegro (Boehm, 1984); the Nuer of Sudan (e.g., Evans-Pritchard, 1940); the Yanomamö and Jívaro of the Amazon (Chagnon, 1977; Harner, 1972); the Tausug of the Philippines (Kiefer, 1972); the Swat Pathan (Barth, 1959) and Pukhtun (Lindholm, 1982) of Pakistan; the Plains Indians of North America (see, e.g., Lowie, 1954); the settlers and frontiersmen of the nineteenth-century American South and West (Ayers, 1984; McGrath, 1984); medieval Icelanders (Miller, 1990); and early modern European aristocrats (e.g., Stone, 1965: chap. 5). Honor assumes different—sometimes very different—forms in each of these societies, but it always manifests itself in a strong concern with maintaining a reputation for courage and aggressiveness before the court of public opinion.[1]

"Jealous in honor, sudden and quick in quarrel" is Shakespeare's summary of this moral system (*As You Like It*, act 2, scene 7). And indeed the hallmark of honor is a heightened sensitivity to insult coupled with a belligerence in responding to it. Honor cultures tend to be egalitarian yet competitive. Social standing is precarious; people must be constantly alert to being put down. What in one culture might be shrugged off as impoliteness, in an honor culture will be deemed a serious attack on character. In Sudan, for instance: "A Nuer will at once fight if he considers that he has been insulted, and they are very sensitive and easily take offense" (Evans-Pritchard, 1940: 151).

A very different setting—nineteenth-century America—exhibited similar patterns:

> The insult, real or presumed, explicit or uncertain, about women or anything else was the classic call to a Southern duel. . . . To insinuate that a man used the truth loosely, or make disparaging remarks about a man's family, friends, business, church, political beliefs, status in society, or physical appearance was to invite a challenge.
>
> (Williams, 1980: 21)

Later in the century, in the mining towns on the western frontier, "disputes over who was the better man . . . careless insults, and challenges to pecking order in the saloon" were common precipitators of lethal conflict (McGrath, 1984: 253). And among the farming people of highland Montenegro most interfamily feuds arose out of insults to honor whether verbally expressed or implied by conduct (e.g., the seduction of an unmarried girl) (Boehm, 1984: 103).

In honor cultures, people are shunned and criticized not for exacting vengeance but for failing to do so. For instance, in the highlands of Albania:

Public opinion . . . spurred the avenger on. A man slow to kill his
enemy was thought "disgraced" and was described as "low class"
and "bad." Among the Highlanders he risked finding that other men
had contemptuously come to sleep with his wife, his daughter could
not marry into a "good" family and his son must marry a "bad" girl.
. . . His coffee cup was only half-filled, and before being handed to
him it was passed under the host's left arm, or even his left leg, to re-
mind him of his disgrace. He was often mocked openly.

(Hasluck, 1954: 231–232)

People who retaliate, by contrast, acquire prestige. "You went
up the hill a boy and came down a man" (Gilsenan, 1976: 201).
Compliments of this kind (paid to a Lebanese man who went to
an elevated section of his village and killed his cousin's enemy)
are found where honor reigns, and they reflect the respect enjoyed by those who employ appropriate violence. Among the Jívaro of the Amazon, for instance, vengeance killers gain the
prestigious reputation of *kakaram* (i.e., powerful one) (Harner,
1972: 112). The Swat Pathan of Pakistan require any man who
aspires to being a chief to demonstrate his valor by murdering
his enemies (Barth, 1959: 85–86). And of the eighteenth-century
Anglo-Irish aristocracy it was said that "no one could take his
proper station in life until he had 'smelt powder'" (quoted in
Kiernan, 1988: 107).

Honor makes people touchy. Incidents that to outsiders appear to be relatively minor may nonetheless precipitate a forceful response. In one case in Albania, for instance, an argument
about the relative size of the first stars to appear in the evening
sky led to a feud in which seventeen people were killed and
eleven wounded (Durham, 1909: 131). "The triviality of many
disputes" was a characteristic of European dueling as well
(Kiernan, 1988: 117). In 1803, for instance, a Captain MacNa-
mara killed a Lieutenant-Colonel Montgomery in a duel triggered by a skirmish between their dogs in Hyde Park, London.
And the duel that Handel fought in 1704 originated in a disagreement over nothing more momentous than who should play
the harpsichord (Kiernan, 1988: 122).

Honorable people are especially touchy in the presence of others. An anthropologist who studied the Tausug of the Philippines, for example, relates that he witnessed several friendly fist fights that became "deadly serious after a crowd gathered and the participants became sensitive to appearing cowardly before an audience" (Kiefer, 1972: 55). Likewise, audiences and public opinion played an integral part in the antebellum southern duel (Williams, 1980). If a gentleman was queried about a remark he had made, he had to state publicly that it was not intended as an insult in order to avert a challenge. Should a gentleman decline the challenge of a duel, he could expect his opponent to "post" his refusal on posters or in newspapers (Williams, 1980: 44–49). At the duel itself, the presence of spectators was an integral part of the procedure. Their number was usually small, but large crowds of observers, many wagering on the outcome, were not unknown either. For instance, more than four hundred people showed up for a duel in Clinton, Mississippi, in 1836 (Williams, 1980: 55).

Honor also makes people verbally aggressive. Just as status can be lost by accepting insults, so it can be gained by issuing them. The Montenegrans, for instance, are said not only to have "a low personal tolerance for insults" but also to exhibit "a strong tendency to insult other people in the name of manly fearlessness" (Boehm, 1984: 103). Verbal pugnacity is a feature of most honor settings. A colorful example comes from Savannah, Georgia, in the early years of the nineteenth century, where the local newspaper described a citizen as a man with a "'contracted phiz and phlegmatic constitution; the features of his countenance appear clouded with malignant passion; his soul is prone to false invective; and though the insidious smile should now and then relax the furrows of his brow it bears no claim to benevolence'" (quoted in Williams, 1980: 22).

Insults can be much more subtle, posing dangers for the visitor unschooled in local custom as well as dilemmas for the insider familiar with the etiquette of honor. Part of the give-and-take of honor cultures, their "dialectic of challenge and riposte" as one sociologist puts it (Bourdieu, 1966: 197), is that people issue ambiguous affronts that force the recipient to choose between appearing excessively sensitive, on the one hand, or insufficiently manly, on the other (Pitt-Rivers, 1966: 28). Insults, equivocal and otherwise, allow rivals to probe and test each other for weakness, feeling out who is, and who is not, prepared to stand up for himself, to fight. This mixture of sensitivity toward the self coupled with competitiveness toward others is a potent one. It renders honor cultures unusually prone to violence that erupts suddenly yet may endure for years.

Honor, finally, is passionate. Quick to anger, quick to love is a common motif in honor cultures. The antithesis of middle-class rationality, honor is warm, generous, and impulsive. Honor is the morality not of the bureaucrat or accountant but the warrior and aristocrat. Sometimes, as in early modern Europe and the antebellum American South, it is bound up with an ethos of hospitality, hard drinking, and gambling (Kiernan, 1988; Wyatt-Brown, 1982: chap. 13). In and of themselves leisure, alcohol, and betting are compatible with a high degree of peace and order. But in settings dominated by honor, they add fuel to the smoldering fire, compounding the predisposition toward bravado, display, and violence.

## *Modern Honor*

Opinions about modern honor have changed considerably in recent years. Not long ago, three eminent sociologists wrote of the "obsolescence of the concept of honor" (Berger, Berger, and Kellner, 1973: 83–96). That view is no longer widely shared. Breaches of honor—sometimes known as disrespect or "dissing"—are at the root of much violence in modern societies, a fact more recent writers have come to emphasize (see, e.g., Horowitz, 1983; Black, 1993a; Butterfield, 1995; Courtwright, 1996).

The Social Location of Honor

Honor is, however, obsolescent for certain groups, especially the middle and upper classes. Individuals who are integrated into jobs and families and whose youth is behind them are seldom concerned with developing a reputation for physical bravery. For them, honor has "no resonance, no meaning" (Ayers, 1984: 13). They value dignity, which in principle accords all persons equal intrinsic worth, regardless of how others view them. A culture of dignity expects people to ignore rather than to confront insult, to cultivate inner strength rather than outward display, and to let the state rather than the aggrieved prosecute violence (Berger, Berger, and Kellner, 1973: 83–96; Ayers, 1984: 19–33).

But honor has not disappeared from modern society; it has just moved down the social pyramid.[2] As Peter's case described at the beginning of the chapter suggests, honor remains central to the lives of the young and the poor (e.g., Daly and Wilson, 1988: chap. 6; Polk, 1994: chap. 4). Marvin Wolfgang observed in his study of Philadelphia homicide that

> The significance of a jostle, a slightly derogatory remark, or the appearance of a weapon in the hands of an adversary are stimuli differentially perceived and interpreted by . . . lower socio-economic males of both races. A male is usually expected to defend the name and honor of his mother, the virtue of womanhood (even though his female companion for the evening may be an entirely new acquaintance and/or a prostitute), and to accept no derogation about his race (even from a member of his own race), his age, or his masculinity.
>
> (1958: 188–189)

Honor today is not necessarily identical to its classical counterpart. Modern honor is, for example, surrounded by less formality than aristocratic honor, and is more individuated and less collective than honor in feuding societies. Nevertheless, honor retains the same core, laying out a code of conduct that commands the use of violence in certain situations (see, e.g., Canada, 1995). This code was well summarized by a young black man from an impoverished, inner-city, all-black neighborhood I interviewed as part of my Virginia study: "Don't be pushed around; if somebody insults, or hits you, or steals your property, don't go to the police, get even. Hit back."

Not all lower-status people participate equally in the culture of honor (Anderson, 1994). The young and the single are more involved than the old and the married; men more than women (indeed honor is sometimes equated with manliness). Lower-status people also differ in how they relate to the culture. Some embrace it willingly, passing on to the younger generation the maxims by which they lead their own lives: "'Protect yourself.' 'Don't punk out.' 'If somebody messes with you, you got to pay them back.' 'If someone disses you, you got to straighten them out'" (Anderson, 1994: 86). Others abhor the culture of honor but, surrounded by it, must come to terms with it. As a survival tactic, parents may therefore teach their children to retaliate, though they would prefer their children did not to have to face a violent world at all (Canada, 1995: chap. 1).

## Maintaining a Reputation

As in days gone by, maintaining a public reputation for fearlessness is a central consideration for those located within a modern culture of honor (see, e.g., Horowitz, 1983: chap. 5). An honorable person must display heart, must not only be prepared to fight but be seen to, for in the competitive world of honor others will create tests: "There are always people around looking for a fight to increase their share of respect" (Anderson, 1994: 88). Turning the other cheek does no good, avoiding confrontation now will only attract more later. Word that somebody can be taunted or pushed around will inevitably spread. It is therefore far better in the long run to fight and lose than not to fight at all (Canada, 1995: 16).

The importance of reputation maintenance can be seen most clearly in the role that audiences play in violence. A lot of modern violence is enacted in the presence of other people. One of the things that struck Donaldson (1993: 70), for example, about the lower-income public housing project in New York that he observed was the sight of "people sprinting from all sides to get a look at a fight. A fistfight is topnotch entertainment." Nor do these audiences just passively observe the fight; often, they urge the disputants on. In an incident in New York City, for example, a group of teenagers exhorted one of their peers who pulled a gun on another boy after a dance to "pop [shoot] him, pop him" (Canada, 1995: 116). The armed teenager did not take the advice, but many who kill are egged on by an encouraging audience. A California study of murderous conflicts found that in more than 40 percent of cases members of the audience "actively encouraged the use of violence." They did this in several ways, including "indicating to opponents the initial improprieties, cheering them toward violent action, [and] blocking the encounter from outside interference" (Luckenbill, 1977: 183–184). A New York study made similar findings (Felson and Steadman, 1983).

Audiences do not always encourage violence. They can be a source of peace. Where a culture of nonviolence exists, the mere presence of third parties is likely to dissuade the principals from coming to blows. In cultures other than honor cultures, public violence is neither appreciated nor frequent. It is when people are concerned with acquiring or maintaining a reputation for courage that the addition of an audience promotes violence (see, e.g., Suttles, 1968: 81–82). Thus, Oliver's (1994: 103) interviews with low-income black men involved in barroom violence revealed that many of them believed that in the presence of an audience it "was important to act in a way that would deter others from attempting to take advantage of them in the future." Or as a man convicted of killing another in a fight said with reference to the onlookers who were present, "I can't have them around here calling me a coward" (quoted in Levi, 1980: 291).

Audiences can also promote the verbal aggressiveness sometimes found in honorable locations. Among low-income African Americans, a stylized trading of mutual insults in front of others—"the dozens"—is a long-established custom. Each party tries to devise insults, preferably in the form of rhymed couplets, deprecating the other person's character or family. The object is to outdo the opponent before an appreciative audience. Rhymes often target mothers and are commonly sexual in nature, as in the following example:

> I hate to talk about your mama
> She's a sweet old soul
> She's got a rap-pa-tap-pa tap dick
> And a pussy hole.
> Listen mother fucker
> You a two-timing bitch
> You got a ring around your pussy
> Make an old man rich.
> (Quoted in Majors and Billson, 1992: 94)

The dozens is a game, played for enjoyment. Most of the time it is just that—fun. But it can turn nasty. If a party is humiliated, subjected to insults that are just too close to the bone, the exchange can become physical, ending in a fight or even a death (Canada, 1995: 52). In a culture of honor where everybody needs to look tough, swapping insults, however humorous, is a risky business.

## Triggering Incidents

Many disputes about honor continue to be triggered by comparatively minor incidents. People have been known to kill in response to a remark about somebody's clothing, a dispute over a few cents of change, a glance directed at another's companion. Honor killings involving passionate and sudden ripostes to reputational slights are especially likely to occur outside the family, between nonintimates (see, e.g., Luckenbill, 1977; Daly and Wilson, 1988: chap. 6; Polk, 1994: chap. 4).

Many people—particularly those who belong to a culture of dignity—regard disputes about honor as incomprehensible, absurd, appropriate grist for the satirist's mill (see, e.g., Amis, 1989: 24). What strikes them is the triviality of the parties' grievances, evidence, perhaps, of how cheap life is among the poor.

The charge of triviality misses the point. A man who grew up in a working-class African-American neighborhood in Virginia, for example, recalls that:

> Some of the most brutal battles I saw in the streets stemmed from seemingly petty stuff. . . . But the underlying issue was always respect. You could ask a guy, "Damn, man, why did you bust that dude in the head with a pipe?"
>
> And he might say, "The motherfucker disrespected me!"
>
> That was explanation enough. It wasn't even necessary to explain how the guy had disrespected him. It was universally understood that if a dude got disrespected, he had to do what he had to do.
>
> (McCall, 1994: 55)

Thus, the deeper problem in honor disputes is nearly always that of respect, and respect is vital when a reputation for strength or vulnerability quickly becomes public knowledge and largely determines how others will treat one. (For this reason, as the historian Edward Ayers [1984: 274] has noted, a white southern aristocrat of the nineteenth-century would probably better understand the violent conflicts of young, lower-income males than do most middle-class people today.) Consider the following case, for instance. It occurred between two young black males, longtime acquaintances, in a cafe-lounge in Houston, Texas. The description is taken from the killer's statement to the police after the victim, who had a reputation in the neighborhood for being tough, had died of multiple stab wounds:

> Clifton came over and sat at the table where I was sitting. About five minutes later some food that I had ordered was served. Clifton asked for some of it and I gave him two pieces of meat and a slice of bread. We were sitting there eating together and he asked me for another piece and I gave him another piece. He got through with that piece and he then reached over in my plate and got another piece [without asking]. I told him to put it back on my plate and he got mad and

put it back. I got up from the table and was going over to another table when Clifton splashed hot sauce on my clothes. I asked him why he did that and he told me that he would do it again and about this time he got hold of the neck of the bottle like he was going to hit me with it. He came at me with the bottle and I pulled my knife out and as he grabbed me I cut him. His brother grabbed a chair and he was going to hit me with it. Some of the people in the lounge grabbed the chair from him and he then took Clifton to the hospital.

(Quoted in Lundsgaarde, 1977: 111)

To the parties themselves, the real issue in this case was not the food but the open insult implied by the taking and spilling of the food. Once they embarked on a public contest over dominance and submission, the killer and victim moved into an escalating sequence of challenge and defiance from which they never escaped. Neither party could back down and still preserve honor.

And yet there is a strand of truth in the claim that honor disputes are often trivial. In many other settings, this disagreement either would not have arisen or been shrugged off; certainly it would never have resulted in a homicide. Nowhere do people like or profit from being publicly insulted, but only in honor settings does public insult routinely result in violent retaliation. Because honor accrues to those who put others down yet resist being put down themselves, people become quick to see and avenge insult. Honor creates violence by lowering the standards of necessary provocation. Many honor conflicts, are, therefore, objectively, less provoked. For the student of violence, the critical task is to figure out what social conditions foster honor. In the remainder of the chapter I discuss two third-party conditions that appear to increase the salience of honor.[3]

## Tie Stability

Honor—both modern and classical—is characterized, then, by several features, among the most prominent of which is the keen pride people take in how they appear in the eyes of others. But for pride to matter so much, third-party ties must be relatively stable and enduring. If ties are too fluid, public opinion is unlikely to become the powerful force that it is in honor cultures. Hence, honor flourishes in social settings in which third parties have stable ties to the principals and to one another.[4]

Stated thus, the link between stable ties, honor, and violence may seem obvious but in fact it is not. Stable ties are often thought to have the opposite effect—to promote peace (see, e.g., Shaw and McKay, 1969). When people are united by bonds that endure over time, the argument runs, antisocial, selfish behavior decreases. This view has been challenged. Black (1993a) argues that immobility is one of the social characteristics of a "stable agglomeration"—the social environment or field in which vengeance flourishes (see also Baumgartner, 1988; Cooney, 1998). Whatever the effect of stability in general, it does appear that third-party stability boosts the importance of reputation. In that way, third-party stability can foster violence, while third-party fluidity inhibits it.

The argument can be summarized in the following proposition:

*Violence increases with the stability of third-party ties.*

Third-party stability explains why, today, honor is found among lower-status men in urban areas, most of whom live in densely populated neighborhoods in which everybody knows or knows of everybody else. Information about people circulates quickly and easily. A writer who spent a year observing a public housing project in New York noticed that

> the environment of a housing project is so hypersocial that people get to know each other fast and well. There are so many chances to do good, bad, or nothing that each person writes his résumé every day right in front of his neighbors. . . . Nothing in Brownsville and East New York is done alone. The people who live there know it. . . . The great and small moments of their lives are performed in front of witnesses. (Donaldson, 1993: 159–160)

An even more stable setting is prison (Black, 1993a: 77). News of strength and weakness travels fast behind bars. Prisoners quickly learn who is and is not aggressive in responding to slights (Abbott, 1981). The weak get picked upon; the strong are left alone or pick on others (Silberman, 1995). To project a forceful, uncompromising demeanor helps to keep predators at bay and to discourage others from starting quarrels. But demeanor must ultimately be backed up by actions. Other inmates will eventually discover whether a tough-looking prisoner is prepared to fight when insulted, attacked, or preyed upon. A prisoner who is not will lose respect and be exploited. To survive with honor intact, then, a prison inmate must "maintain a truculent exterior, beware of insult, and always be ready to fight" (Butterfield, 1995: 108).

By contrast, honor is rarely found in settings where social ties are more fluid and interchangeable. Thus, hunter-gatherers are rarely obsessed by honor (Nisbett and Cohen, 1996: 5). Their mobile way of life militates against it. In the face of conflict, members of hunter-gatherer groups can escape their enemies by moving elsewhere; they do not have to stand and fight (Black, 1993a: 79–83). Moreover, because everybody is in flux, nobody has to create and maintain a reputation for toughness. The same is true of modern suburbanites (Baumgartner, 1988). Again, the high turnover of relationships and the privacy of suburbs means that news of how people handle conflict does not circulate among a stable collection of people, rendering a concern with honor moot and violence rare.

This is not to imply that all relationally stable settings have an honor culture, however. Many small towns and villages are both stable and peaceful and their residents do not seek to become known for their fearlessness. Other factors must be at work in creating a concern with honor.[5] The next section analyzes a second third-party foundation of honor: statelessness.

## Statelessness

Statelessness, it may be recalled, arises under three conditions: when legal officials are either nonexistent, too low, or too high in status relative to the principals. When there is no state, statelessness is actual; when the law is of insufficient status or of too high status, statelessness is virtual. All forms of statelessness tend to promote honor because a reputation for fearlessness helps to keep would-be aggressors away when disputants cannot or will not call on the state for protection (Nisbett and Cohen, 1996: 7). Virtual statelessness, moreover, fosters honor indirectly—as a reaction to the social distance and status superiority or inferiority of legal officials. Police and prosecutors today belong to a high-status world that is often remote from the experience of the socially disadvantaged. In earlier times, officials belonged to a world significantly lower in status than that of the elite. Both scenarios generate opposition by disputants to the intervention of legal officials.

Statelessness, then, is associated with another set of characteristics of honor: conflict with the law. For honor, at least in its pure form, is not neutral with respect to legal authority; it resents, struggles against, and sometimes manipulates law.[6]

### Honor and Law

In an influential discussion of honor in Mediterranean societies, Julian Pitt-Rivers makes the point that

> the conflict between honor and legality is a fundamental one which persists to this day. For to go to law for redress is to confess publicly that you have been wronged and the demonstration of your vulnerability places your honor in jeopardy, a jeopardy from which the "satisfaction" of legal compensation at the hands of a secular authority hardly redeems it.　(1966: 30)

Pitt-Rivers goes on to say that this applies equally to the aristocrat who is above the law and the slum dweller who is outside it.

Of the two groups mentioned by Pitt-Rivers, little is known about aristocrats' relationship with the law. An attitude of lofty disdain is evident, for example, in the petition a nobleman wrote to King Louis XIV of France to complain of the ban on dueling when he argued that a man of his nobility ought not to have to place his honor in the hands of "menial lawyers" (Kiernan, 1988: 55). But a detailed account of aristocratic adjustment to the law remains to be written.

Much more has been learned about the relationship between low-status people and the law. It is clear, for instance, that low-status groups, such as impoverished minorities, often seek to exclude the law from their conflicts and resent what they see as its interference in their affairs. Legal officials are well aware of this. They can see it in the cold stare they get from young black men—"eyefucking," as the Baltimore police call it (Simon, 1991). They can see it in the contempt and disrespect with which they are often treated by the public (Black, 1971). And, above all, they can see it in the lack of cooperation that greets their efforts to solve crimes (see, e.g, Canada, 1995: 128–130). Thus, their requests for information are commonly met with blank denials of knowledge, even by those who were obviously present at the scene of the incident. One study of detectives, for instance, describes a homicide in which a person was shot to death in a crowded bar in the presence of one hundred people. Not a single person voluntarily came forward to testify (Waegel 1981: 269–270).

The intimidation of witnesses partly explains why people are slow to provide the police with information or courts with testimony. In a Washington, D.C., study more than one-quarter (28 percent) of the witnesses said that they feared reprisals (Cannavale and Falcon, 1976: 55–56). A similar study in Brooklyn Criminal Court, New York, discovered that two out of every five witnesses were afraid of revenge and one in four had actually been threatened (Davis, Russell, and Kunreuther, 1980, cited in Graham, 1985: 4).

Yet intimidation alone is insufficient to account for the lack of cooperation police receive from members of lower-income minority groups, as a study carried out in London, England, reveals. In England, West Indians have a niche similar to that occupied by African Americans in the United States: a racial minority, they are disproportionately poor, unemployed, and have lower-than-average educational attainment (see, e.g., Runnymede Trust and Radical Statistics Race Group, 1980). Against this background, two English researchers developed a survey posing three hypothetical crime scenarios and asking respondents whether they would be prepared to give evidence in court if they witnessed the incidents. People of West Indian extraction said they would be prepared to identify the offender to the police and to testify in court less frequently than whites.[7] They also said that they would be less willing to tell the police what they had seen even if it did not involve identifying the offender. The authors conclude that "reluctance to help among West Indians does not arise primarily because of fear of reprisals from the offenders" but because "they tend to be more antipathetic or hostile to the police than other groups" (Smith and Gray, 1985: 178).

## Legal Hostility in Modern America

Low-status antipathy to the law is easily documented. The writer James Baldwin, for example, vividly described how many lower-income African Americans perceive the police:

> Harlem is policed like occupied territory . . . [and] what I have said about Harlem is true of Chicago, Detroit, Washington, Philadelphia, Los Angeles, and San Francisco—is true of every northern city with a large Negro population. And the police are simply the hired enemies of this population. They are present to keep the Negro in his place. . . . To respect the law, in the context in which the American Negro finds himself, is simply to surrender his self-respect. (1966: 417, 420–421)

A more recent resident of Harlem echoes these sentiments: "Police have little or no legitimacy in poor communities" (Canada, 1995: 128). Similarly, a writer who spent two years observing Brownsville, New York, a low-income, predominately black section of New York City, remarks that "police as a group are simply despised here" (Donaldson, 1993: 95). In south-central Los Angeles, a former gang member writes that "nothing but hostility" exists between the police and young black men (Shakur, 1993: 65). And a resident of the poor, African-American section of San Francisco argues that the police are "an occupying force" whose motto "to protect and to serve" might be more accurately phrased "to accuse and to abuse" (Marshall and Wheeler, 1996: 78).

Surveys consistently reveal that low-status people hold more negative views about the police and the legal system in general than do other groups. In a study conducted in Utah during the 1970s, for instance, 70 percent of the urban poor and minority respondents held unfavorable attitudes toward the police, compared to only 40 percent of urban middle-class respondents (Albrecht and Green, 1977). A Texas survey published in the early 1980s reported that Latinos were twice as likely to express dissatisfaction with the police as the rest of the population (Carter, 1983). And a national survey conducted in 1992 found that the poor, nonwhites, and less educated people expressed less confidence in the ethics, impartiality, and honesty of the criminal justice system in general and the police in particular (Maguire, Pastore, and Flanagan, 1993: 169–172).

When low-income people do summon the police, typically they do not get the response they want. An observation study conducted in three large U.S. cities found, for example, that the lower the social status of the parties, the less care and attention the police devote to their disputes (Black, 1980: chap. 5). Consider, for example, the following case from New York City. A man who grew up in a poor, minority community recalls how when he was seven years old, his nine-year-old brother was robbed on the street:

> We called the police. We couldn't afford to lose ten dollars. They took their time coming and I'm pretty sure were quite amused at this naive family, so serious about catching a thief in the South Bronx. This contact with the police shook my confidence in the world.

Something was terribly wrong here. It was nothing they did, it was what they didn't do. They didn't take us seriously. They came because they had to come. They asked questions not because they thought the answers might help catch the thief, but because they had to do something when we were so insistent. I looked at the two white officers and realized that while their mouths were saying one thing, their manner and attitude were saying something else. We can't believe you made us walk up all these stairs for a lousy robbery of ten dollars. What's the matter with you people, don't you know where you live? We'll come because we have to, but we don't have to do anything. You're on your own.

The lesson was straightforward and clear. The police didn't care. This lesson would be reinforced again and again as I grew older. It would be more than twenty years before I would call them again. Like many others trapped in the ghettos of this country, I had learned that police are not the answer when trouble comes to your door.                                                 (Canada, 1995: 14)

If the police are called and do take action, they tend to use a restricted set of remedies in cases involving low-status parties. Where low-income blacks, for instance, are concerned, "the police seem to vacillate between indifference and hostility. . . . [R]eluctant to become involved in their affairs yet heavy-handed when they do so" (Black, 1980: 139). Should the police seek to reconcile the principals, they typically invest less time and energy in devising a solution than in cases between high-status parties. Nor is this pattern confined to police: prosecutors and courts tend to be equally uninterested in the disputes of low-status people, typically disposing of them quickly and, to the parties involved, unsatisfactorily (see, e.g., Feeley, 1979; McBarnet, 1981).

By contrast, the law does not have the same punitive edge for the middle and upper classes; in times of trouble, it is a help, not a hindrance. When they call the police, they tend to get what they want, be it official recognition that a crime has occurred or the arrest of a suspect (Black, 1970, 1971). If they have interpersonal disputes, the police are likely to relate to them in a remedial rather than an accusatory manner. Officers will sometimes devote hours to these cases, perhaps even involving several of their colleagues in the search for a solution acceptable to the parties, something virtually unheard of when low-status people are involved (Black, 1980: 134–147). Moreover, if the police do not provide satisfaction, there are other legal outlets available. Elites are more likely to invoke and receive favorable treatment from other legal officials as well, such as prosecutors, lawyers, and judges (see Black, 1976: 16–30; Baumgartner, 1992: 142–148).

## Legal Hostility in Other Societies

Lower-income African Americans are far from being unique in their hostility to the law. Low-status groups everywhere tend to have tense relationships with legal officials. For example, a survey of thirteen European countries found that the lower the social class of the respondent, the less positively he or she viewed the law. Poorer and less educated people were significantly less likely to express support for the law and to believe in its neutrality than those above them in the social hierarchy (Gibson and Caldeira, 1996).

One of the ways in which lower-status people communicate their hostility toward the law is in resisting the state's involvement in a case, its tendency to take over the conflict (Christie, 1977). Consider for example, Finland's most prominent low-status group, the Gypsies. When a homicide occurs, Gypsies eschew all reliance on police and prosecutors, seeking instead to exact vengeance by killing the killer or one of the killer's close relatives. Should the authorities get involved in a blood feud, Gypsies will not cooperate and will even actively mislead them. An anthropologist who studied the Gypsies comments that the Gypsies will do everything in their power to keep the law out of a case, including engaging in "refusals to testify, deliberate misleading of the authorities, and general non-cooperation with the Finnish judicial agents" (Grönfors, 1986: 107–108).

Highland Albanians similarly resist the intrusion of the state into their system of blood vengeance. In one case, a woman took every opportunity to criticize her husband's brother for killing her husband. But when the police arrived and questioned her, she lied, telling them that the shooting was an accident. For this, "she was openly commended by the public for preventing the government from shaming her husband's family by arresting the murderer" (Hasluck, 1954: 211).

Historical examples can be cited as well. In nineteenth-century Ireland, for instance, the native Irish were generally much poorer and less educated than the colonial English who ran the state and the legal system. This was especially true of the impoverished native-speaking peasants in rural areas. These people were notoriously reticent when legal officials came seeking information about cases. In one murder case in 1882 when three farmers did come forward with testimony, it was said that "such a thing had never quite happened before in Ireland" (Waldron, 1992: 35).

In nineteenth-century America, minority groups in the mining towns on the western frontier exhibited a similar reluctance to cooperate with the law. Mexican and Chinese immigrants were more inclined to seek justice through vengeance than through legal channels. The authorities found it difficult to get members of these groups to provide information or testimony if the perpetrator was one of their own (McGrath, 1989: 140). In one case, for instance,

> hundreds of rounds were fired during [a] battle and at least one Chinese was killed and several others seriously wounded. Witnesses said that another three or four Chinese had been killed but their bodies had been carried away before police arrived. Some thirty Chinese were arrested and eight were charged with murder. However, one by one the charges were dropped for lack of evidence. It was simply impossible to get any Chinese to testify. Nor was anything ever learned about the bodies that were supposedly carried away.
>
> (McGrath, 1989: 140)

This pattern persists. Residents of New York's Chinatown in the late twentieth century are similarly slow to testify in legal cases (Kinkead, 1992: 74–76).

## Manipulating the Law

But the law can be strong and tenacious. Sometimes it intrudes into cases despite people's best efforts to keep it out. When it does, one common response is for the litigants to manipulate the legal process for their own private ends. Thus, honorable people may incorporate law as a weapon in the struggle against their enemies. The nomadic, camel-herding people of Somalia are adept at this. Forbidden by the authorities from carrying on their traditional feuds, clans preparing a raid sometimes leak information of the planned attack to the police but move the actual attack forward a few days. "The forces of law and order then tend to arrive after the assailant had struck and just as the outraged group is preparing its reprisal" (Lewis, 1961: 29).

Legal manipulation is also practiced by the Tausug of the Philippines. Primarily resident on the island of Jolo, the Tausug are a Moslem minority in a predominately Christian nation. Relations between the Tausug and legal officials range from the tense to the outright rebellious. Thomas Kiefer (1972: 138), an anthropologist who studied the Tausug, states that their antipathy to the law is such that "the average Tausug man in most rural areas would rather die than submit himself to Philippine justice." The Tausug will, however, often take out criminal warrants on their enemies, thereby ensuring that the government as well as they are seeking the individual concerned. As Kiefer (1972: 139) notes, "enemies use warrants of arrest against each other in somewhat the same way as they use bullets." But the Tausug will not otherwise cooperate with the legal system. The result is that while the legal system is clogged with warrants, most murder cases go unsolved for lack of evidence because witnesses almost invariably refuse to testify, preferring to exact vengeance themselves. In short, "the Philippine system of justice simply does not work in Jolo except as an unwitting supplement to traditional Tausug justice" (Kiefer, 1972: 139).

The corollary of legal manipulation is that what cases are said to be about is probably not what they are really about. In a sense this is true of many legal conflicts. Under the guise of a contract case, for example, business rivals may seek to settle personal scores that have been festering between them for years. But in the case of manipulative legal action, the contrast between official and actual reality is likely to be especially stark. False witnesses may be recruited, documents forged, and bribes tendered, all in an effort to keep a friend from prison or to send an enemy away for something he or she did that is not the focus of the trial. Consider, for example, the legal sequel to Tom's case described at the beginning of chapter 1 (in which George killed a man in a fight arising out of a bicycle):

> Some months later, the police arrested Tom for the killing. But of the 100 or so people who, Tom estimated, witnessed the event only one came forward. The witness was the victim's girlfriend, who tentatively identified Tom. He flatly denied the charge. Although encouraged by the police to reveal the identity of the killer, he insisted that he knew nothing about the homicide. When the prosecutor went ahead with the case, Tom arranged with his brother and best friend to provide an alibi. But the witnesses themselves had felony convictions and were not called by the defense lawyer. The jury brought in a guilty verdict after a police officer testified about information he had received about Tom's involvement.

In this instance, the legal case is but a continuation of the street conflict. This seems to be common enough among virtually stateless people who find themselves largely outside the protection of the law. If their cases do make it to court, both sides may arrange for their witnesses to testify—untruthfully, if necessary—to a benign version of the facts (see, e.g., Shakur, 1993: 24, 27, 157–158).

To be sure, lies may be told in any case. The parties to corporate litigation, for example, can be extremely proficient at covering up facts and misleading legal officials. Additionally, corporations are often able to attract expert witnesses to testify in their favor. Litigation between people involved in honor disputes therefore has no monopoly on presenting radically different versions of the facts. Nonetheless, in legal disputes involving the honorable (e.g., gang members) the factual claims made often appear to be unusually divergent, the telling of lies more direct, and the manipulation of the legal system for private ends less subtle.

Overall, then, the relationship between the law and honor is complex. Pure honor disdains the law. But honor may be mixed with dignity, and the law may be highly developed. Consequently, the state may intrude into honor disputes. When it does, the honorable may use the law aggressively and even enthusiastically to harass their enemies. Despite their natural antipathy to the whole legal process, people involved in violent disputes about honor may, under some conditions, actually be the most frequent users of the courts (see, e.g., Blee and Billings, 1996).[8]

Much violence, then, in modern and premodern societies arises out of a culture of honor or respect. Honor is a warrior ethic quite distinct from the morality of dignity that prevails in the office towers, shopping malls, and suburban homes populated by the middle and upper classes. Yet honor lives on among the young, the poor, the unconventional, and the disreputable. Honor has moved down but not out of the status hierarchy. As in days gone by, the principal features of honor are that it is a (1) a rule-bound moral system that (2) values a public reputation for (3) bravery (4) into which children are socialized and under which people are (5) sensitive to insult, (6) verbally aggressive, and (7) quick to retaliate for (8) provocations that are often objectively minor; a system that generates (9) hostility to law and, sometimes, (10) a willingness to manipulate legal officials and institutions to further private disputes. Although some systems of honor have more and some fewer, these characteristics form the core of honor systems everywhere. They rest on several social foundations, two of which are third-party effects: relational stability and statelessness.

# 6

## Conclusion

More than four hundred years ago, the English writer John Donne ([1624] 1959: 108) coined the famous aphorism "No man is an island." Donne's simple statement expresses not just a human truth but a working sociological principle: To understand people's actions, look at those around them, the groups familiar with their affairs, the kinds of networks in which they are enmeshed. Human behavior is not the result of individual decisions alone; it is profoundly influenced by other people, the advice and support they give, the manner and style in which they intervene, the enthusiasm or indifference they exhibit toward different acts.

Violence is no exception to the powerful effect of others. Although scholars have concentrated overwhelmingly on the role of the principals and the macroenvironment in explaining violence, third parties commonly dictate the course conflict takes. Third parties can bring peace to the most violent of disputes, persuading belligerent antagonists to lay down their arms and talk out their differences. Or they can urge irresolute disputants to take offense and to fight, thereby causing the most innocuous of disagreements to flare up into prolonged feuding. At times, their influence—whether as warriors, peacemakers, or something in between—is patent and obvious even to the most casual observer. At other times, it is more subtle, concealed by what appear initially to be principal or macroenvironmental effects. On either occasion, it must be addressed if violence is to be fully explained.

As time goes by, third parties are likely to become increasingly central in the study of violence. There are at least three sets of reasons that third parties deserve more attention than they have generally received: their implications for researching, reducing, and explaining violence.

## Researching Violence

Third-party research is still in its early stages. Previous chapters have documented a variety of ways in which the actions and inactions of family members, friends, neighbors, onlookers, and legal officials can promote violent or nonviolent outcomes to conflict, but, clearly, there is considerably more to be learned.

### Additional Third-Party Effects

Consider, for example, the U-curved idea presented in chapter 2. That proposition predicts that violence is high when third parties are high above or lower than the principals in social status. Among the findings that would falsify the proposition are (1) settings in which third parties are considerably higher in status than disputants do not have more violence than settings in which third parties are only moderately higher in status; (2) when third parties are outranked in status by some disputants, violence is no more common than when third parties outrank all disputants; (3) in modern societies, low-status people are not involved in violence, as offenders and victims, more often than their numbers in the population predict; and (4) in earlier and simpler societies, high-status people killed and were killed in conflict no more frequently than they are today. Moreover, the proposition raises several other research questions. For instance, in medieval and early modern Europe were elites more, less, or about as violent as those at the bottom of the social pyramid? The U-curved proposition does not provide a definite prediction: Because elites were above the law and the poor and dispossessed were outside the law, both ends of the curve could be found within the same society, and it is not clear which should produce the greater violence.

The tie configurations discussed in chapter 4 provide further research opportunities. Of all the configurations that are empirically possible, data are available on relatively few. What happens, for example, when third parties are relationally close to one side and distant from the other side but are members of an organized group to which both principals belong? Or when third parties are relationally distant from both sides but, again, are members of an organized group to which both principals belong? Although there are no data on these possibilities, Black's theory of partisanship allows us to make some predictions about these hybrid cases. But the theory runs out in other cases. For instance, how likely is violence when one set of third parties is organized but the other is not?

Then there are other third-party variables. Black (1993b: 126) argues that cultural distance has effects on partisanship similar to those of relational distance. Hence, all else the same, third parties should support principals who belong to the same ethnicity, race, religion, or linguistic group as themselves and tend to oppose those who belong to different cultural groups. Though plausible, systematic evidence for this proposition is lacking.

Another aspect of the theory of partisanship focuses on social status. Black (1993b: 127) proposes that "partisanship is a joint function of the social superiority of one side and the social inferiority of the other." This proposition predicts that third parties will gravitate toward the higher-status principal and that the higher the status of the principal relative to the other principal, the more support the third party will provide. In terms of partisanship, then, the rich get richer and poor get poorer. Again, though plausible on its face and consistent with the way other spheres of social life operate (Merton, 1968), there is, as yet, not much empirical evidence to support this idea. Moreover, the effect of status partisanship on violence has not been explored.[1]

There is also scope for more macrosociological research. As

discussed in chapter 4, close and distant group ties tend to produce reciprocal violence, and close and distant individual ties tend to produce unreciprocated violence. But where do these configurations of ties themselves come from? At one level, they might be seen simply as naturally occurring phenomena, as the product of haphazard historical development. But that does not explain why these configurations are concentrated in low-status neighborhoods today. Conflict configurations are not randomly distributed throughout the social hierarchy. Ultimately, then, the origins of the networks from which conflict configurations spring must be documented and explained.

Finally, while this book argues that the status and ties of third parties explain interpersonal violence in general, the data on which the argument draws mainly relate to lethal violence. Outside the domestic sphere there are few studies of violent conflict that do not result in death. The third-party propositions provide a set of hypotheses for predicting the conditions under which nonlethal violence occurs. If they are correct, and if nonlethal violence is simply a less extreme form of violence, third-party status and ties associated with lethal violence should be found in less intense form when the violence is nonlethal.[2]

## Conflict

Black's (1983) insight that violence is a form of morality contains several underexplored empirical implications. One is to turn attention away from crime to conflict. Instead of being seen as a type of social pathology, violence is, for this perspective, a means of handling conflict found under certain social structural conditions. Hence, in place of looking at what violence has in common with, say, shoplifting, the researcher seeks to situate it in the context of other ways in which people handle conflict. Some conflict behavior is criminal, but most is not. A conflict perspective therefore changes the landscape of violence; it creates a new set of comparisons and contrasts (Black, 1998).

Consider, for instance, the role of parents in the violent conflicts of their children. Criminological theory holds that children who are close to their parents will be less likely to turn to crime than those who are distant from their parents (Hirschi, 1969). While the theory works quite well for many crimes, such as theft, robbery, burglary, drug taking, and prostitution (Krohn, 1995), it may not hold for assault and homicide. As we have seen, in honor cultures—including virtually stateless locations in modern societies—parents must often train their children to hit back. Many parents do this reluctantly; they neither like violence nor want to see their children getting into fights and incurring the risk of injury or death. (Thus, parental support for their children's violent acts may not show up on a survey.) But without a general climate of peace, parents cannot afford to teach their children a consistent ethic of nonviolence. As long as honor remains a strong concern, most parents will recognize the reality that violent retaliation is not optional but mandatory if the child is to flourish rather than merely survive. Under these conditions, then, close ties to parents are likely to be consistent with certain types of violence, though not with other types of crime.

Viewing violence in terms of conflicts over right and wrong inevitably leads the researcher beyond third parties. In Black's theoretical paradigm, the status and ties of the principal parties are just as crucial a component as those of third parties. Consider, for example, the role of relational distance. A considerable proportion of violence occurs between intimate principals, especially when rates of violence are low (Daly and Wilson, 1988). Yet there is also reason to believe that, all else the same, violence is more likely to be lethal when it occurs between non-intimates. The ratio of lethal to nonlethal violence in marital relationships, for instance, is vastly lower than among more relationally distant people (Zimring, Mukherjee, and Van Winkle, 1983: 924–925). These opposing effects warrant further investigation.

## Beyond Official Data

Much criminological research on violence employs official data gathered by the police or other criminal justice agencies. These data have proved to be extremely useful, and a great deal has been learned from them. But official data have their limitations; understandably so: criminal justice agencies gather information primarily to catch and convict criminals, not to understand violence as a natural phenomenon. Hence, official files often contain little information on issues that do not bear directly on guilt or innocence but that are nonetheless sociologically relevant. Much third-party behavior, for example, receives little official coverage because it contributes to the evolution of lethal violence without necessarily involving any legal culpability.

To expand our understanding of violence, it is necessary to make more use of other sources of information. Looking beyond official data allows the researcher to trace the origins and development of conflict in greater detail. Here there is much to learn from the anthropologists, who have long obtained high-quality information on violent incidents. Only rarely have anthropologists been in a position to observe homicides or feuds for themselves, but with the help of informants they have carefully reconstructed the unfolding of conflicts and the role played by the various dramatis personae. The results are in-depth case histories rarely found in studies of modern violence. When it comes to nuance and richness of detail, more, strangely, is known about preindustrial than modern violence.

In developing richer accounts of violent conflicts, surveys can be helpful; so too can controlled experiments, whether conducted in the laboratory or the field. But the most valid information is likely to come from ethnographic work. Ethnography allows the student of violence to record or reconstruct the status and ties of the principals and third parties in the kind of detail that is required to understand cases fully.

Comparative Studies

More comparative studies would undoubtedly increase our understanding of violence. One kind of study would compare settings with high and low levels of violence. In the previous chapters I have on several occasions contrasted Baumgartner's (1988) suburban study with data on inner-city violence. Valuable though this contrast is, more studies are needed. The problem is that there are few systematic investigations of conflict among nonviolent groups (but see, e.g., Ellickson, 1991; Morrill, 1995). Consider university students, for example. By some indicators, students ought to have a lot of violent conflict. They are at a peak age for violence, free of parental control, and are loosely integrated into family and work life. Yet there appears to be comparatively little violence and certainly little lethal violence among them. A study of conflict management among students that allowed comparisons to be drawn with their same-age peers in inner-city neighborhoods would, in all likelihood, add considerably to our knowledge.

Comparisons of low-status communities themselves provide another possible line of inquiry. Some low-income settings generate high levels of violent conflict; others do not. Thus, homicide rates vary significantly across low-income ethnic and racial minority groups in America. Latinos, for instance, generally have less violent conflict than African Americans. Why is this? Why do some disadvantaged groups and settings manage to limit violence more successfully than others? Do third parties play a significant role?

Cross-cultural and cross-national studies also have considerable research potential. But these need to go beyond analyses of the macrostructural features of different societies (e.g., how unequally income is distributed). After all, societies are not violent; particular people and groups within societies are. Of especial interest, then, would be detailed comparisons of conflict management among the most violence-prone groups—low-status people—in societies with high and low rates of violence. Why, for instance, do young men from impoverished backgrounds in urban America have so much more lethal violence than their counterparts in England or Japan? What exactly is different about the social contexts of their conflicts? How do third parties figure into those differences?

## Reducing Violence

The goals of this book are primarily programmatic—to encourage greater scholarly interest in third parties—and theoretical—to explain findings in the research literature. Nevertheless, the study of third parties has implications for another issue: the reduction of violence. In this section I briefly consider how third parties might be deployed to promote more peaceful outcomes to conflict.

Some third-party conflict structures are easier to manipulate for peaceful ends than others. The third-party configurations discussed in chapter 4, for instance, are products of the closeness and distance found in naturally occurring social networks and groups. They typically involve a whole series of people: family members, friends, acquaintances, enemies. Complex and subtle, they do not easily lend themselves to external change.

Settlement offers more promise, however. Settlement is often effected by a single person or small group. While it may emerge from everyday relationships, it is often created, altered, and eliminated by conscious design from above or outside. As such, it appears to be more easily manipulated to achieve desired ends.

### Theoretical Reprise

If third parties are to promote the peaceful settlement of conflict, they should neither be too low nor too high in status relative to the principals. Third parties who are too low—lower in status than the principals—will not command the respect of disputants (Black and Baumgartner, 1983: 113). They will not be sought out in times of strife and, if they are, their words will not be heeded. People want settlement agents whom they admire; they want to look up to those to whom they submit their disputes. When settlement agents are not at least their social equals, they will, like the aristocrats of old, reject the third party's jurisdiction and handle conflict themselves. Violence will increase.

But disputants do not want third parties who are too high in relative status either. As (Black, 1993b: chap. 8) observes, vertically distant third parties have a strong tendency to be moralistic. They eschew consultation, compromise, and conciliation in favor of control, commands, and coercion. Disputants do not like to be treated in this unforgiving manner, and they will reject settlement agents who belong to a distant high-status world. Without settlement agents, they are likely to develop an honor culture that emphasizes toughness and sensitivity to insult. Many socially disadvantaged people today find themselves in precisely this position: they have a hostile relationship with the legal system and its officials that renders them virtually stateless. As a result, they sometimes turn to violence to settle their differences.

Relational distance has a similar effect. Third parties who are equally relationally distant from the principals tend to be either indifferent or coercive toward the disputants. Their natural inclination is not to get involved, to remain aloof (Black, 1993b: 134). But if they do intervene (e.g., because it is their job to so) they typically do not exhibit much sympathy for or understanding of the principals (Black, 1993b: chap. 8). They relate to conflict in terms of abstract rules and declare absolute winners and losers. They do not investigate the causes of the conflict in any real depth, and their rulings are commonly harsh and punitive. They too are often rejected by disputants, again fostering a concern with honor and rendering violent resolutions more frequent.

To promote peace, then, settlement agents must have relatively specific characteristics. They must be slightly higher in status and relatively intimate with the principals. Settlement agents who answer these requirements ought to command both the approval and respect of disputants, regardless of whether they are state officials, private individuals, or a hybrid of both.

Socially close third parties are an increasingly familiar phenomenon in many countries, and it should therefore be possible to create a corps of third parties with these specific violence-inhibiting characteristics. In the remainder of the section I outline the contours of a system of popular justice built around two types of a socially close third party: "elders" and "peacemakers." Because the system is primarily designed to reduce violence among the urban poor, I call it "street justice." The system can be implemented in different ways by different communities, and hence it makes little sense to try to legislate all its detailed workings. What follows, then, is a sketch of the principal features of street justice. These features draw on several models already in existence, as well as on more general proposals for decentralizing law and criminal justice (for the latter, see, e.g., Danzig, 1973; Black and Baumgartner, 1980; Black, 1989: chap. 5).

## Elders

The role of community elders would be to establish and staff tribunals dedicated to settling disputes in a consultative manner. Elders would be a new type of "old head," men and women from the same or a similar community who understand the rules prevailing there and work out a solution consistent with it and the wishes of the principals. As their name implies, they would have some seniority, but they would not constitute a gerontocracy. Exceptional people in their twenties might become elders if they commanded enough respect from those in their midst.

Elders would be invested with wide discretionary powers but would have no jurisdiction to imprison. They could, for example, arrange restitution either to the victim personally (e.g., in a robbery case) or to the community as a whole (e.g., in a gunfight that endangered children). Payment could take the form of

money, or work, or both. They could bring the principals together, trying to get to the root of the disagreement, encouraging
apology and mutual recognition of wrongdoing, where appropriate. For people involved in long-term relationships, they could
arrange counseling or other therapeutic services. For other disputants, they might even recommend controlled violence as a solution. In some conflicts between belligerent teenagers, for example, the elders might conclude that the best prospect for long-
term peace lies in having the antagonists box or wrestle under
supervision at a gymnasium. If they did, and the disputants
agreed, the parties could in effect duel their way to an honorable
but minimally dangerous outcome. The general point is that the
rulings of elders' courts would emphasize consensual solutions,
flexibly tailored to suit the demands of particular cases.

Use of elders' tribunals would be optional, but failure to use
them would bring the parties into the regular court system. The
courts might even provide incentives for disputants to use the elders' tribunals by, for example, increasing the penalties for those
who could have but did not invoke the elders.

Something similar to elders tribunals already exists. Perhaps
the closest analogy is the community mediation centers that have
sprung up in the United States and elsewhere since the 1970s
(see, e.g., Merry and Milner, 1993). In community mediation,
members of the public provide an alternative to courts by serving as mediators for disputants in their community who wish to
reach consensual settlements. Experience has shown that community mediation is generally liked by disputants once they try it
(see, e.g., Merry and Silbey, 1984; Pearson and Thoennes, 1985).
However, few disputants use it voluntarily, with the result that it
usually depends on courts for case referrals (see, e.g., Harrington, 1984, 1985; Morrill and McKee, 1993). Moreover, from the
point of view of reducing violence, community mediation suffers
from a second limitation: it happens too late. Violence, by its nature, is often quick and impulsive, and its prevention therefore
requires on-the-spot intervention.

Similar strengths and weaknesses attach to another form of decentralized dispute settlement that has been implemented in many countries in recent years: restorative justice (see, e.g., Wright, 1982; Wright and Galaway, 1989; Cragg, 1992). Restorative justice—also known as reconciliation (see, e.g., Umbreit, 1985) or peacemaking (see, e.g., Pepinsky and Quinney, 1991)—seeks to return conflicts to the parties themselves by bringing offenders and victims together (Christie, 1977). That goal can be achieved through a variety of formats (Launay and Murray, 1989). One common model employs the services of a mediator who encourages the principals to express their feelings about the crime and to achieve some measure of reconciliation through the completion of restitution, either monetary or nonmonetary (see, e.g., Umbreit, 1989). An alternative model is the accountability conference held when the perpetrator of a criminal offense admits his or her guilt (Braithwaite and Pettit, 1994). The offender and victim are both assisted by friends and family members. There is no mediator, just a facilitator. The conference takes the form of a problem-solving dialogue, focusing on the ways in which the offender can remedy the harm he or she caused the victim.

Restorative justice appears to result in high rates of offender compliance with restitution agreements and to be well received by the general public (see, e.g., the essays in Messmer and Otto, 1992). Elders' tribunals would do well to learn from it. However, restorative justice is not suitable for ongoing disputes in which the parties do not admit fault. It is also powerless to deal with most violence before it is committed.

In short, there are models already in existence on which elders' tribunals could draw. But experience with these new forms of decentralized settlement suggests that, by themselves, they are of limited use in reducing violence. Hence, the need for the second corps of third parties: peacemakers.

Peacemakers

Peacemakers would be members of the local community trained to intervene quickly in disputes in order to prevent them from escalating into violence. Peacemakers take the currently popular idea of community policing (see, e.g., Greene and Mastrofski, 1988) a step further by making communities, at least to some degree, self-policing. A pilot program of this kind has already been implemented among young people in the Harlem section of New York City, apparently with some success (Canada, 1995: 158, 160–161). One of its creators—Geoffrey Canada—suggests expanding the idea nationwide. The following discussion draws on Canada's proposal but goes beyond it in not confining it to youth violence.

Peacemakers are essential because, as we have seen, violent conflicts commonly have short life spans, evolving quickly from confrontation to assault. Successful peacemaking is therefore frequently a rough-and-ready business, often consisting of nothing more elaborate than third parties stepping between people about to come to blows or pulling them apart after they have already done so. Simple though it is, this third-party intervention interrupts the escalation process. Today, the diminution of close ties means that peacemaking of this kind is less common than it once was. Increasingly, the public expects the police to prevent and break up fights. But the police are not very effective in doing so. They typically arrive too late, after the injury or death has already been inflicted. The problem is not so much that the police are sluggish in responding to calls for help but that citizens are slow to call them when fights break out (Caplan, 1976, as discussed in Manning, 1977: 215–216). The lack of trust that residents of poor and minority communities have in the law often means that even when altercations take place in public before many witnesses nobody is prepared to summon the police. Confrontations can then escalate under their own momentum, free of external restraint or persuasion, up to and even beyond the point of lethal violence.

The essence of the peacemakers proposal, then, is to make available to the urban poor the services of trustworthy third parties who can intervene speedily in conflicts. Unlike most police, peacemakers would be members of the community (or one similar to it) and be familiar with local customs. Of different ages, they might be community organizers, former gang members, former convicts, or local sports stars. The only qualifications they need are to be able to command the personal respect of those around them and to be committed to resolving conflict nonviolently. A criminal record or a violent history need not preclude a person's becoming a peacemaker. In fact, it might be an advantage. Gang members, for instance, may listen to people who have never been in a gang, but they may well not.

Peacemakers could be advocates for nonviolence, participating in community- and school-based violence prevention programs (see United States Department of Justice, 1994). But their central task would be to circulate in their communities, keeping an eye out for disputes. To perform that difficult and sometimes dangerous task, peacemakers would be trained in how to defuse and mediate conflict. They would not be armed and would have no jurisdiction to imprison, punish, or coerce anybody (other than physically restraining him or her from attacking another person). They could work alone or in groups, as circumstances dictate. They would patrol the community, actively seeking out conflicts likely to explode into violence. They would hang out with gangs who have been attacked, for instance, seeking to dissuade them from exacting vengeance. Adult officers could talk to couples with domestic problems. They would try to settle the dispute themselves or persuade the principals to appear before an elders' court for a more thorough airing of the grievances.

No doubt there would be cases where the peacemakers were not called, where they would arrive too late to prevent a violent altercation, or where their attempts to settle would fail. But there would also surely be instances where their intervention would make all the difference between peace and violence, even between life and death. Moreover, they would not stand alone. They would be the first, but not the last, line of defense against violent conflict. They would be assisted by the community elders, for whom they would provide a source of cases.

Additional Issues

Many additional issues would have to be worked out before a system of street justice could be implemented. One is the relationship between street and criminal justice. There is a continuum of possibilities. At one extreme, street justice could simply supplement the law. For example, peacemakers might accompany police on patrol, helping them do their job more effectively by acting as go-betweens in police-citizens interaction. At the other extreme, street justice could replace the law altogether so that legal officials and institutions would have no jurisdiction in certain communities unless invited to do so.

All solutions have their drawbacks. The supplementary model runs the risk that since it changes nothing, nothing will change. Street justice would, in all likelihood, be looked upon as a public relations exercise on the part of the police, rather than as a serious attempt to put communities in charge of their own affairs. However, the replacement model runs the risk that the withdrawal of the law—especially if sudden—among people long accustomed to it could increase violent conflict before the new system established itself (see Baumgartner, 1992: 29–31).

Additionally, without legal oversight the system of street justice could be open to abuse of various kinds. But limiting the role of the law is no easy task; once involved, lawyers tend to take over things. The challenge would be to give the law a part without letting it dominate. How that balance is to be achieved is best worked out in practice, with different communities experimenting with different formats.[3]

The same point applies to several other issues (e.g., how many elders should hear cases; how conflicts between members of different street justice communities should be decided). These could and indeed should be determined on a trial-and-error basis. What works in America might not work in, say, Nigeria.

Flexibility also extends to terminology. The terms "street justice," "peacemakers," "elders," and "elders' tribunals" may not be acceptable to the people for whom the strategy is intended.

The terms are just initial suggestions, open to revision and replacement. The best people to give labels to street officials and institutions are the people affected and employed by them.

Street justice is not a panacea. No matter how well it works, it is likely to experience an enduring tension between the need to settle cases informally while still respecting the formal rights of citizens. Moreover, imperfections and breakdowns are, as in every system of justice, inevitable. But good communication among systems of street justice would help to maximize success and minimize failure over time.

Street justice would require money. Buildings would have to be rented, equipment purchased, and salaries paid. This is not the place to address the practical question of how to meet these expenses. But present arrangements are themselves costly. Violence deepens divisions between people, creates fear, deters productive and sociable activity, and devours large chunks of medical and criminal justice resources. By moving funds to violence prevention, street justice could, quite conceivably, result in overall savings. After all, preventing an evil is typically cheaper than curing it. Why should violence be any different? Moreover, the strategy ought to have several other benefits that would have to be kept in mind in weighing its desirability:

- Street justice provides a nonrepressive means of controlling violence. Some people argue that to reduce violence, it is necessary to get tough on it: hire more police officers, reduce procedural protections for individuals accused of crime, impose longer sentences, build more prisons, make parole harder to obtain.

  These solutions rarely work. The most severe punishment of all—the death penalty—has no deterrent effect, at least as currently administered (see, e.g., Paternoster, 1991: chap. 7). Punishing domestically violent men with short spells in jail deters some from hitting their wives, but it makes others even more violent (Sherman, 1992). This is not to say that measures taken by police and other criminal justice agencies are always ineffective (see, e.g., Meares and Kahan, 1997). But repressive measures are ultimately of limited use. As we have seen, much violence arises because of hostility toward the legal system. Increasing punishment—the burden of which will invariably fall on the socially disadvantaged—is likely only to enhance resentment of the law and all that it represents. The outcome may well be more violence, not less.

- Street justice encourages lower-status people and communities to find their own, local solutions to violence. It represents a bottom-up rather than a top-down solution. Like the idea of community mediation, it should appeal broadly to people of different political persuasions (see, e.g., Harrington and Merry, 1988).
- Street justice creates jobs in disadvantaged neighborhoods. Moreover, the jobs it would provide are socially useful: dispute settlement is a highly valued function in all human societies.
- Street justice does not require utopian change, be it sociological (redistributing societal wealth) or psychological (altering violent personalities). Because it draws on decentralizing trends already in motion, it should be workable.

## Summary

Sociologists, as sociologists, have no business telling people what moral or political positions they should take. Hence, this discussion does not advocate, and should not be taken to advocate, the implementation of a system of street justice. Yet sociologists will readily acknowledge that many people espouse the goal of reducing violence. Street justice is a means of realizing that goal.

Settlement declines and violence flourishes when third parties are too high or low in relative social status and too distant relationally. As things now stand, many low-status groups today correctly view police officers and judges as the agents of a distant and hostile elite. A system of street justice would make available two types of third party who are vertically and relationally close to disputants, and who belong to the same world. Peacemakers and elders would alter the third-party structure of disputes, increasing the probability of honorable yet peaceful resolutions of conflict. Street justice would draw on existing trends in criminal justice, bringing several developments already under way within a single program. For that reason, street justice appears to be a realistic approach to the problem of violence.

## Explaining Violence

Regardless of whether street justice were to be implemented or effective, third parties have implications, finally, for explaining violence. Black's theoretical paradigm provides the most integrated and comprehensive treatment of the roles third parties play in conflict. As we have seen, a core feature of the paradigm is the emphasis it places on viewing phenomena in their widest possible perspective. Third parties reveal why cross-cultural and historical materials are not just an exotic appendage but a vital component of the scientific understanding of violence.

### The Virtues of Generality

The central reason for taking cross-cultural and historical data seriously is that they are indispensable to the construction of general theories. General theory is the ultimate goal of scientific thinking. As Black (1995: 833) puts it, "[S]cience craves generality." Thus, biologists, as a group, try to understand the evolution of all living things, not just human evolution. Astrophysicists address variation in all celestial bodies, not just those in the vicinity of the earth. Why should theories of violence be confined to one type of society, be they modern, historical, or tribal? Not that every study of violence has to be explicitly cross-cultural. There will always be a need for detailed analyses of single settings. But if the study of violence is to be truly scientific, empirical investigations must feed into a body of general theory that seeks to explain violence wherever and whenever it occurs.

Material from earlier and structurally simpler societies has the further advantage of revealing the limitations of some popular explanations of violence. Guns and media violence, for instance, are wholly absent from some societies that have very high rates of violence (e.g., the Gebusi). Similarly, the decline of religion and the growth of urban anonymity cannot be considered fundamental causes in light of the sharp drop in European rates of violence since medieval times.

Finally, there is a third, more subtle, reason that cross-cultural and historical data are important: without them, empirical and theoretical scholarship may present a misleading, even distorted, picture of violence. As things now stand, the social study of violence is split into several strongly demarcated disciplines. Each discipline has its own traditions, methodologies, skills, seminal works, theories, and findings. But what most defines the disciplines is that they study violence in a particular kind of society. Anthropology concentrates on structurally simple societies, history on the societies of the past, sociology and criminology on modern societies. The problem is that the patterns discovered by each of these disciplines, no matter how strong, are not necessarily found in the other types of society. Consider inequality, for example. Inequality is a strong predictor of modern violence, and is routinely invoked by criminologists to explain variation in homicide rates. But it does not predict violence in simple, preindustrial societies (Rosenfeld and Messner, 1991). The dynamics of inequality and violence differ in the two types of society. The same may well be true of other factors that explain modern homicide. Only through cross-cultural inquiry can we learn which criminological patterns are products of modernity and which are of more general validity.

If patterns of violence vary across different types of society, then theories of violence that are not cross-cultural and historical in scope are likely to be of limited, though unknown, applicability. The material discussed in chapter 2 provides a good example. Because the great bulk of modern violence occurs among the socially disadvantaged, most criminological theories are designed to explain a tight connection between violence and low social status, at least as they are currently formulated (Tittle, 1983). As a result, those theories are not well positioned to explain the historical and cross-cultural fact of elite violence and its gradual decline over time. Anomie theory, for example, explains violence with a culture of normlessness (Merton, 1940; Messner and Rosenfeld, 1994). But elite violence often enforced general social norms, and sometimes was itself governed by explicit norms (e.g., dueling). Strain theory proposes that violence is a response to the frustration of blocked opportunity or other negative social-psychological experiences (Henry and Short, 1954; Blau and Blau, 1982; Agnew, 1992). But aristocrats were not blocked from getting ahead, and their conflicts were negative enough to result in violence only at one time and not later. Subcultural theory holds that values promoting the use of violence held by particular (usually low-status) groups explain violence (e.g., Miller, 1958; Wolfgang and Ferracuti, 1967). But in earlier and simpler societies violence was found among all groups. Why, then, did it later become restricted to particular subcultures? Social disorganization theory contends that violence is found in communities that lack internal solidarity as a result of poverty, heterogeneity, and mobility (Shaw and McKay, 1969; Sampson and Groves, 1989). But feuding communities are typically culturally homogenous and stable. Control theory asserts that violence is a product of the weak control exerted by the self and others when social ties attenuate (Hirschi, 1969; Gottfredson and Hirschi, 1990). But elites who feuded in stateless agricultural societies belonged to exceptionally strong families and communities. Differential association theory (Sutherland, 1947) and social learning theory (see, e.g., Akers, 1985) locate the explanation of violence in attitudes and behavior acquired from others. But they do not explain why elites no longer exhibit attitudes and behavior conducive to lethal violence.

Few of these anomalies are necessarily insurmountable. Some, perhaps all, of the theories could be modified or extended in order to explain the decline of violence among social elites. However, were they to do so, they would be significantly different. They would no longer be just theories of criminal violence. They would be theories of violence in general.

General theories are surely the way of the future. Theoretical studies of violence other than Black's have begun to address an increasingly broad range of social contexts. Daly and Wilson's (1988) evolutionary psychology theory, for instance, draws widely on cross-cultural and historical data. Tedeschi and Felson's (1994) social-psychological theory of aggression likewise incorporates references to material from earlier and structurally simpler societies (see also Felson and Tedeschi, 1993). In the years to come, this trend seems likely to intensify.

## Transcending Crime and Deviance

General theories require general concepts. Because the concept of crime is limited to state societies, it impedes the formulation of general theory. Realizing this, scholars have occasionally sought to make criminology more universal by expanding the concept of crime (see, e.g., Schwendinger and Schwendinger, 1970). But their laudable efforts have typically run into the problem of relying on moral judgements as to what should be considered crime (Lynch and Groves, 1989: 32–33). Perhaps the time has come, as Black (1994, 1998) argues, to abandon the concept of crime as a theoretical category altogether. (Because it makes the modernist assumption that violence is not the socially approved means of responding to insult or injury, the broader concept of deviance is not entirely satisfactory either.) Not only is it too narrow, it is also too broad, including a miscellany of behaviors that are very different from one another. Criminal homicide, for instance, encompasses actions as diverse as infanticide, lethal barroom altercations, serial slaying, killing through drunk driving, and gang feuding.

Crime is, after all, a legal and administrative category. It should not be expected to provide a sound basis for a scientific discipline. As the world comes closer together and demand for global theory increases, a future generation of scholars is likely to find it increasingly restrictive. The Blackian concept of conflict provides an alternative that both reflects the underlying ethnographic realities of behavior the state defines as criminal and that facilitates analysis transcending space and time. If this and other general concepts are adopted, the boundaries between criminology, anthropology, history, and other disciplines will likely wither away, but the science(s) that replaces them will yield a more accurate picture of the world and a fuller explanation of the human experience.

# Appendix A
*Moralistic Homicide*

What percentage of murders is moralistic and what percentage is predatory? Since no records are kept precisely on the point, there is no definitive answer. However, a considerable body of evidence, from America and elsewhere, indicates that in all societies for which we have information most homicides are moralistic.

## America

Two large data sets suggest that between 60 and 80 percent of homicides in the United States are of the moralistic variety. The first is Maxfield's (1989) analysis of the circumstances of homicide described in the Supplementary Homicide Reports for 1976–1985. The Reports are produced by the FBI from information supplied by local law enforcement agencies across the nation. Maxfield calculates that approximately 60 percent of all homicides are conflict homicides and 40 percent instrumental or, in our terms, predatory. However, it is likely that the percentage of homicides that are moralistic in the sense used here is higher than 60 percent for three reasons. First, as Maxfield (1989: 691) acknowledges, there is evidence that some of the 13 percent of homicides classified by the FBI as predatory "felony" homicides actually originate in conflict because while the killer steals from the victim, he or she does so after, and incidentally to, the killing. Second, although Maxfield (1989: 679) treats both the 2 percent of gang and 1 percent of drug-related homicides as predatory, most of these have a characteristic shared by other forms of moralistic homicide: they are primarily committed between people with a prior relationship (see 1989: 678, table 3). Third, while Maxfield is probably correct that most of the "unknown" (17 percent) and "other felony" (7 percent) homicides are predatory, almost 20 percent of both are committed between people with a prior relationship, and hence at least some are likely to be moralistic.[1]

The second source of information is the Chicago Homicide Dataset. The dataset provides information on all homicides reported to the police in that city from 1965 to the present; through 1993, there were more than 22,000 included. The dataset classifies homicides as instrumental (i.e., committed to acquire money or property) or expressive (i.e., committed to perpetrate violence itself), a distinction that corresponds approximately to the predatory-moralistic dichotomy. The great majority of Chicago homicides are expressive. From 1965 to 1990, only 19 percent of homicides were instrumental. Not enough is known about an additional 17 percent to permit a categorization (Block and Christakos, 1995). However, even if all the unknown homicides were predatory, that would still mean that 64 percent (i.e., about two out of every three) of Chicago homicides are moralistic.

## Other Societies

In other societies, the percentage of moralistic homicide is usually higher than in the United States. In Canada, of the 12,828 murders known to police in the years 1961–1990, approximately 75 arose out of conflicts (a percentage, it might be noted, that would probably be even higher had manslaughters been counted) (Silverman and Kennedy, 1993: 9, 55). Polk's (1994) study of all homicides committed over five years (1985–1989) in the Australian state of Victoria reveals that about 3 out of every 4 are moralistic (calculated from 1994:

23).[2] Bohannan (1960b: 249) classified the motives for killing, as revealed by legal records, for a sample of 100 homicides from each of two Ugandan tribes, the Gisu and the Soga, using Wolfgang's (1958) motive categories. Although these categories are far from perfect (Daly and Wilson, 1988: 170–174), it is significant that for the Gisu, none of the cases were clearly predatory, and for the Soga, only 3 percent were. Studies of Indian tribal groups find similar patterns. Categorizing the motives in 100 cases that resulted in a conviction for homicide among the Maria Gond, Elwin (1950: 51) found that 5 arose out of insanity and 8 out of robbery or robbery accusations. The remaining 87 all appear to have been moralistic killings. A study of the Munda and Oraon tribes and other castes and communities in the Ranchi district of India reports that while the motive for murder was obscure in 11 percent of the 598 cases, only 3 percent were clearly predatory (1 percent of cases were homicides committed for gain, and a further 2 percent were human sacrifices) (Saran, 1974: 70). Qualitative ethnographic evidence supports these results. The vast majority of killings described by anthropologists arise out of disputes over honor, sexual fidelity, prior homicides and the like (see, e.g., Hasluck, 1954; Barth, 1959; Kiefer, 1972; Koch, 1974; Rosaldo, 1980; Boehm, 1984; Ginat, 1987).

Moralistic homicide also appears to have dominated in earlier societies. Given (1977: 106), in a study based on court records, found that in thirteenth-century England of 2,434 victims, only 9 percent were killed in robbery-murders. Analyzing coroner's records from a century later, Hanawalt (1979: 171) reports that 20 percent of all 459 homicides in Northamptonshire and London in the years 1300–1415 were robbery-murders; the remaining 80 percent were moralistic.

Whatever the setting, then, homicide appears to be predominately a moralistic act.

# Appendix B
## *The Virginia Study*

In 1989–1990 I interviewed 75 people—63 men and 12 women—incarcerated for homicide in the Virginia prison system. The prisoners were serving sentences ranging from five years to death.

After receiving permission to conduct the interviews, the Department of Corrections supplied me with a roster of all people admitted to the system for homicide in 1988, listed by inmate number. From the list of 208 numbers, I randomly drew a sample of 50. When I required more interviews, I sampled the remaining numbers in the same manner. The numbers were then grouped according to location, and visits to the sites arranged with the warden of each facility. Eventually I conducted 83 interviews at fifteen sites. Eight of the interviews—typically among the earlier and less informative ones—were discarded, leaving a final sample of 75.

At each correctional institution, I interviewed each of the prisoners in a room, alone, typically in the "treatment center" where the offices of staff psychologists and counselors are located. Twenty-two prisoners declined to be interviewed. As the study progressed, I realized that many of the prisoners wondered why he or she, and not somebody else, had been selected. Consequently, I amended my opening statement to include a remark that his or her number had been "drawn out of a hat." After that, fewer prisoners refused to participate.

During the interview, I tried to set the prisoner at ease. I offered cigarettes to those who smoked. I did not tape-record the interviews because I felt that this would inhibit a group of people already suspicious of outsiders. Instead, I wrote down the interviewee's responses to a detailed questionnaire, while still maintaining as much eye contact as possible. I encouraged the interviewee to speak fully about the issues raised. Like most such instruments, the questionnaire was designed to get the interviewee accustomed to speaking, starting off, for example, with a series of innocuous questions about the prisoner's personal and family background. While a few interviewees remained suspicious and reticent, the great majority were helpful and forthcoming. The most successful interviews were those in which the interviewee appeared to relate to the interview as he or she would to a counseling session. Since many of them had had counseling in prison, they were accustomed to speaking about their cases and their own actions at length. Interviews ranged in duration from one and a quarter hours to more than four hours, with a typical interview lasting about two hours.

The interview embraced four main topics: (1) the prisoner's personal and family background, (2) the history and circumstances of the homicide, (3) the informal response to the prisoner and the prisoner's family, and (4) the legal dimension of the case.

At the end of the interview, I asked each whether he or she would agree to my contacting a family member to get his or her perspective on the issues discussed in the interview. Fifty of the 75 defendants in the sample agreed. Of these, it was possible to contact 40 by telephone. In two of those cases I conducted separate interviews with two family members, bringing the total number of telephone interviews to 42. The shortest of these interviews was fifteen minutes; the longest was two and a half hours.

To round out my information, I also conducted in-depth, open-ended interviews with three homicide detectives and a homicide prosecutor in Richmond, the state capital.

The final phase of the research consisted of reading each prisoner's Pre-Sentence Investigation Report. The report is typically compiled by a probation officer and is part of the documentation used in sentencing. I was able to obtain the reports on fifty of the prisoners. In the great majority of cases, the report corroborated the prisoner's account of the killing, although there were several instances where it differed.

# Appendix C
## *The Cross-Cultural Study*

My cross-cultural study explored the response to homicide in thirty societies. Anthropologists specializing in cross-cultural studies have devised several standard samples of societies for use by researchers. One of these is the Human Relations Area Files Quality Control Sample (QCS). The QCS is based on the sixty cultural groups distinguished by George P. Murdock, the founder of the Human Relations Area Files, a set of data files containing information from a large number of preindustrial societies, arranged by topic. The cultural groupings cover the entire world and are primarily based on linguistic criteria (see Naroll, 1967; Human Relations Area Files, 1967).

Shortly before I undertook my study (for a doctoral degree), Donald Black and M. P. Baumgartner had explored the possibility of conducting a world survey of social control. To that end, they had drawn a sample of sixty societies by adapting the QCS. Black and Baumgartner selected from each of the sixty cultural groups the society that had the best information on social control. On the advice of Black (who supervised my dissertation), I decided to select every second society in the Black and Baumgartner sample, beginning with a random start. Where I encountered a society for which the information on the social control of homicide was insufficient, I substituted another society from the same cultural group. If no society in that group yielded good information, I selected a society from a neighboring cultural group. (The societies are listed below.)

Unlike most cross-cultural studies, Black and Baumgartner's did not propose simply to compare one society to another. Because the response to any act of deviance often varies significantly within the same society, the study sought information on the handling of cases within ten relationships within each society. I adopted the same principle for my study. The ten relationships were child-parent, parent-child, husband-wife, wife-husband, male acquaintances, female acquaintances, master-subordinate, subordinate-master, brothers, strangers, and local-alien. Thus, the study focused on variation at the case, as well as the societal, level.

For each society I read the original ethnographic material. Using primarily nominal and ordinal-level variables, I coded a considerable amount of information on a variety of subjects, including aspects of the society's social structure (e.g., type of economy, population density, family form, homicide rate), and for each of the ten relationships, the characteristics of the killer and victim and the relationship between them, the circumstances of the killing, third parties and their status and relationship vis-à-vis the principals, and the behavioral response to the killing. The object was to code the typical response to a typical homicide in the relationship concerned.

I obtained adequate information on ninety of the three hundred possible cases (thirty societies by ten relationships). The smallest number of cases yielded by any one society was one and the greatest was eight. The most common relationship coded was a killing between male acquaintances, in part because I used this relationship (typically the one that in most societies attracts the most homicide) as the default relationship when none was specified by the writer.

For three societies (Tiv, Maria Gond, and thirteenth-century England) the data were derived from archival studies of court records of homicide cases. Since only some homicides result in a court case, the information for these societies is necessarily incomplete. However, because the court records often provide a good deal of information about the killing, these studies are valuable in shedding light on homicide in the three societies.

For the remaining societies, the information came from ethnographic investigations conducted by anthropologists and some others (e.g., missionaries). As with all cross-cultural studies, the information obtained is of variable quality. In some instances, the anthropologist carefully compiles information on all homicides committed, discusses their outcome in detail, and generally provides much high-quality information (see, e.g., Lee, 1979). At the other extreme, the information consists primarily of rule statements about what should happen when a homicide occurs. Since rules and behavior do not necessarily match, information of this kind is of uncertain validity (for a thorough discussion of these issues, see Ember et al., 1991). Most of the information obtained fell between these extremes. It was neither as rich and detailed as one would hope nor as incomplete as one might fear.

| Societies | Approximate Time Period |
|---|---|
| Ju/'hoansi | 1935–1970 |
| Plateau Tonga | 1940 |
| Lugbara | 1900 |
| Ashanti | 1900 |
| Tallensi | 1910 |
| Tiv | 1950 |
| Nuer | 1935 |
| Somalia | 1955 |
| Bedouin | 1950 |
| England | 1200–1300 |
| Albania | 1900 |
| Turkey | 1950 |
| Manchu China (with particular reference to Kwantung and Fukien) | 1890 |
| Korea | 1900 |
| Tibet | 1930 |

| | |
|---|---|
| Albania | 1900 |
| Turkey | 1950 |
| Maria Gond | 1930 |
| Ifugao | 1910 |
| Murngin | 1930 |
| Jalé | 1955–1965 |
| Yapese | 1880 |
| Samoa | 1925 |
| Eskimos | 1955 |
| Tlingit | 1880 |
| Cheyenne | 1840–1860 |
| Chiapas, Mexico | 1960 |
| Jívaro | 1970 |
| Qolla | 1970 |
| Ona | 1870 |
| Shavante | 1960 |
| Yanomamaö | 1970 |

# Notes

1. In the interest of confidentiality, names of the participants in all of the cases narrated in the first-person singular in this book have been changed.

1. An earlier version of this chapter appeared in Cooney (1997b).

2. Some scholars argue that elites today do perpetrate homicide, but because of their social status, it is not defined and treated as "homicide." An example would be the death and injury resulting from industrial activities (e.g., unsafe working conditions). However, while industrial death and injury is an important phenomenon worthy of serious study, it is sufficiently different from death and injury arising from interpersonal violence as to demand separate treatment. It is not "violence" in the sense of aggression, and this book does not address it further.

3. Whether income inequality or poverty better predicts homicide rates is a question much addressed in the research literature. But the question may not warrant the effort put into it. First, focusing on income diverts attention away from wealth, which, of the two, is usually more unequally distributed (see, e.g., Wolff, 1995: 27) and hence may well be a better predictor of homicide than either income inequality or poverty. Second, income inequality and poverty are hard to disentangle. For one thing, they are often too highly correlated to be statistically separated (Land et al., 1990). More fundamentally, poverty is nearly always a relative rather than an absolute concept. For instance, modern definitions of poverty—typically based on governmental criteria—are founded on people's inability to

attain an income level enjoyed by some. "Poverty" in this sense is really a more diffuse kind of inequality.

4. At the aggregate level, the percentage of the population that is unemployed often proves to be statistically insignificant in multivariate analyses (Land et al., 1990: 928–930). However, the unemployed are usually defined as members of the labor force seeking work, a definition that usually excludes those who have given up seeking work and thus have the longest history of joblessness, precisely the most theoretically relevant group. Using the alternative measure of the proportion of individuals aged fifteen to sixty-four who are employed, Shihadeh and Flynn (1996) found that black unemployment is negatively related to black urban homicide.

Residential segregation is another aggregate measure of marginality. In the United States, the residential isolation of blacks from whites increases rates of black homicide (Shihadeh and Flynn, 1996; see also Parker and McCall, 1997; Peterson and Krivo, 1993).

5. Landau and Drapkin (1968: 76) found that 70 percent of persons accused of homicide in Israel, 1950–1964, had not completed primary school. However, they do not report the educational level of the general population.

6. Note that if predatory killings could be excluded from the calculations, the percentage of offenders with criminal records would probably be lower and the percentage of victims would probably be higher.

7. Brownfield (1986) finds that in two self-report studies of nonlethal, juvenile violence, lower-status youths are more violent only under some measures of status (e.g., unemployed father, parents receiving welfare). Note, though, that because virtually all youths have one of the attributes of low status—marginality—a weaker link between violence and the other characteristics of low status is to be expected for teenagers than for adults.

8. In the stateless international realm, the highest-status nations are most heavily involved in warfare (Singer and Small, 1972: 287).

9. Another difference between homicide in modern states and other societies may lie in what Black (1976; 1995) would call its vertical direction. In premodern societies, downward homicide (i.e., committed by higher-status people against lower-status people) seems to have been more common than upward homicide. In modern society, by contrast, upward homicide appears to be more frequent. Consider the United States, where non-Latino whites are, in general, of higher status than Latino whites or blacks. Block (1986: 60), for example, reports that in Chicago, 1965–1982, black-white assault (i.e., conflict-related) homicide was three times more com-

mon than white-black assault homicide. Similarly, Latino-white assault homicide occurred twice as frequently as white-Latino assault homicide (1986: 60).

10. The status of legal officials does not derive wholly from the state, however. Police officers and judges also bring their own status characteristics to their office. Thus, modern elites may be higher in personal status than local police and judges and hence slow to bring cases to them (Baumgartner, 1985). But other legal avenues typically remain open to them, and consequently they do not reject legal authority.

11. Elias ([1939] 1978, [1939] 1982) provides another possible explanation of why elites today react to conflict less violently than those before them, arguing that since medieval times the growth of the state and the development of longer chains of interdependence have increased self-constraint and reduced violence. This long-term process begins among the elite and from there filters down to the rest of the population.

Elias's theory explains the gradual descent of homicide down through the social hierarchy. However, it does not, at least without further elaboration, explain several of the patterns (e.g., the close link between homicide rates and the four dimensions of status inequality). Moreover, it requires evidence on self-constraint, evidence that is difficult to obtain at the best of times, but especially difficult for earlier societies.

NOTES TO CHAPTER 3

1. Some material from this chapter was previously published in Cooney (1997a).

2. Other scholars have argued that although the state may reduce homicide internal to a society, it increases the scale of external warfare, with the overall result that people are more likely to die violently under a state than in its absence (see, e.g., Lee, 1979: 397–399). This argument raises issues beyond the scope of the present book. It appears, however, to be inconsistent with the evidence (Cooney, 1997a).

3. A criticism once made of the data on which these studies are based is that they rarely consist of firsthand evidence and hence reflect more the widespread fear of violence in preindustrial societies than its actual occurrence (Gluckman, 1969: chap. 1; Hoebel, 1971; Moore, 1972; Colson, 1974: 40–43). However, more recent and rigorous evidence, such as violent-mortality statistics and per capita rates of lethal violence, indicates

that violence occurs, sometimes at extremely high levels, in at least some stateless societies (see, e.g., Lee, 1979; Yost, 1981; Knauft, 1985).

4. Some of the lethal violence reduced by colonial states was not "homicide" as defined here but warfare between independent communities.

5. A second factor is sedentarization (see, e.g., Fürer-Haimendorf, 1967: 22). Sedentarization is fateful because it undermines one of the principal peacekeeping mechanisms in hunter-gatherer society, namely, avoidance or the ability of people to move away from one another in times of conflict (Black, 1993a: 82–83).

6. A related point is that preindustrial people who come into contact with, but do not fall under the jurisdiction of, state societies may experience increased internal violence caused by resource depletion and inequality based on unequal access to new goods (Bennett Ross, 1984; Ferguson and Whitehead, 1992; Ferguson, 1995).

7. Note that unlike the comparison between stateless and noncentralized state societies, the comparison between noncentralized and centralized states is not strongly affected by differences in medical resources. In highly centralized regimes, medical care, and adequate food, clothing, and shelter are often deliberately withheld from groups deemed to be enemies of the state. For example, in Cambodia under the Khmer Rouge government, for a doctor to practice medicine among the general population or even to admit that he or she had done so under the previous regime was to invite almost certain death, most likely after prolonged torture (see, e.g., Ngor, 1987). Indeed, in some cases, the best known of which is the Nazi genocide of the Jews, centralized states have employed medical knowledge and personnel to facilitate their mass killing (see, e.g., Lifton, 1986). The absence of medical care for victims of homicide under modern centralized regimes should be seen, therefore, not so much a confounding factor as an indicator of the violent inclinations of the state.

8. The statistics on which Rummel relies are inexact. Thus, some writers, drawing on newly available material, argue that the scale of state repression and killing under the Soviet regime has been considerably exaggerated (Wheatcroft, 1992; Nove, 1993, 1994). Even if this criticism is correct, however, it is clear that highly centralized societies, of which the Soviet Union is but one example, are characterized by rates of state killing that greatly exceed those found in more democratic regimes.

9. Socially disadvantaged groups have variable homicide rates among themselves. For instance, American Indians have a lower rate than African

Americans. Perhaps some of this is due to differences in local hierarchy and settlement within these groups.

1. All parties involved in this case were African Americans.

2. The approach known as network analysis also addresses how variation in social ties explains behavior. For an introduction to the network analysis of crime, see Krohn (1986).

3. For an application of the theory to issues of evidence in legal conflict, see Cooney (1994).

4. Black (1976: 93) treats organizational distance hierarchically, as a difference in status. By contrast, I treat it here as a lateral difference. This allows me to explain partisanship among organizations at the same status level.

5. There is no agreed-upon definition of gangs in the scholarly literature. For an overview of the issues, see Bursik and Grasmick, 1993: 114–123).

6. One common way of limiting violence in these societies is that groups expel any member who commits them to conflict too frequently (Moore, 1972: 89).

7. Knauft (1987) argues that the Gebusi provide an exception to fraternal interest group theory. But, consistent with the theory, the Gebusi do not feud and do not kill one another in interpersonal conflict (Knauft, 1987: 471–473). The Gebusi case suggests that the execution of witches raises some separate issues.

8. At first glance, Lee's (1979: 392) statement that fifteen of twenty-two Ju/'hoansi homicides occurred as parts of feuds seems to contradict the argument. However, most of these "feuds" involved a single act of retaliation for an earlier killing (1979: 383). One conflict did generate nine killings, but most of these arose out of failed attempts to kill a dangerous killer rather than a tit-for-tat exchange of homicide (1979: 390–391).

9. Even the Ju/'hoansi rate seems high compared to modern homicide rates. But recall the caution noted in the previous chapter: because of differences in medicine and technology, considerable caution must be exercised in comparing homicide rates in modern and premodern societies (see also Cooney, 1997a).

10. Waorani kinship classification is known as Dravidian classification (see Kessing, 1975: 105–112).

11. Third parties with ties to both sides may explain an interesting finding in the literature on modern American homicide: that homicides between intimates have fewer witnesses than those between acquaintances and strangers (Zahn and Sagi, 1987: 389–390; Decker, 1993: 605, 607). When intimates have conflicts, the probability that their supporters will have ties to the other side are high. These supporters are likely to intervene to stop the conflict. Intimate homicide occurs, then, when others are not present. On the other hand, when more distant people have conflicts, any third parties present are likely to be either distant from both, in which case they remain neutral as the parties fight, or to have ties to one side only, in which case their support tends to encourage escalation. Homicide between acquaintances and strangers is therefore more likely to take place in the presence of others.

12. Other studies of American homicide report somewhat higher percentages of co-offenders. Thus, Block's study of Chicago homicide indicates that 27 percent of cases involved co-offenders (calculated from 1986: 47, table 2) and a study of murder cases in thirty-three randomly sampled large urban counties found that 33 percent involved more than one offender (Dawson and Boland 1993: 3, table 3). Perhaps urban homicide in the United States is more collective.

13. Since legal officials are employees of the state, they typically have distant organizational ties.

NOTES TO CHAPTER 5

1. The element of public display in honor cultures is also evident in the considerable care and attention men in honor cultures devote to their personal appearance. Honorable men are often dandies with a highly developed aesthetic of the self.

2. American criminologists have long been interested in whether the South has a culture of honor that can help to explain the region's high homicide rate. The empirical evidence is mixed (see, e.g., Stack, 1996). Perhaps the South is too diverse a social unit to harbor a single cultural trait. Work that focuses on specific groups within the South—especially rural whites—appears to be more successful in isolating a culture of honor (Nisbett and Cohen, 1996), though, again, the data are not conclusive (Beck, 1996).

3. Honor can sometimes have spillover effects as well. Maintaining a reputation for toughness often lies behind predatory violence committed by those who belong to a culture of honor (see, e.g., Shakur, 1993: 13).

4. Stability and intimacy, though often found together, are distinct. Ties can be stable but distant (as, for instance, when two enemy groups with very little contact reside long-term in the same location), and fluid but close (as, for example, when highly communal nomadic groups fission and fuse regularly).

5. Nisbett and Cohen (1996) argue that honor thrives in herding economies. While their argument has substance, it does not explain honor among European aristocrats whose wealth derived from agricultural estates.

6. Honor can in principle also arise in opposition to the intervention of nonlegal or informal third parties. However, informal third parties rarely exhibit the same degree of social distance and status superiority or inferiority as legal officials and hence do not typically cause as much conflict with disputants. Consequently, the literature on honor tends to emphasize the struggle between honor and law rather than honor and authority more generally.

7. The authors included two other groups in the survey: Asians and non-West Indian nonwhites. They found that these groups were also less willing to cooperate with the police than whites, although the differences were less marked than with West Indians.

8. One reason is that the close and distant ties that underlie feuding also appear to be conducive to persistent and hostile litigation (Black, 1976). If this is correct, law and feuding have different third-party status characteristics but similar third-party relational and organizational characteristics. Hence, some degree of overlap between law and violence can be expected.

NOTES TO CHAPTER 6

1. There is, however, some evidence on the effects of partisan intervention by a third party on behalf of a principal who enjoys lower social standing or possesses fewer social resources. Third-party support in favor of the lower-status principal appears to discourage the higher-status principal from engaging in violence but may encourage the weaker principal to do so. A recent survey of the preindustrial literature on marital conflict argues

that marriages in which the woman can call on supporters experience less male-on-female violence than those in which she is isolated (Baumgartner, 1993). Data on sibling conflict suggests that when parents punish the older and more dominant child (and thereby side with his or her younger sibling), this increases the overall level of aggression between the children by emboldening the younger child (Felson, 1983; Felson and Russo, 1988).

2. In exploring third-party effects, attention should, in addition, be given to the possibility of nonlinearity. Homicide rates, as we have seen, are subject to extreme fluctuations. Across different societies, they can range from near zero to more than 1,000 per 100,000 (and even higher in the short term). Behind extremely high rates of homicide may lie comparatively small changes in third-party conditions.

3. The point at which a particular community comes to rest on the supplement-replacement continuum will also depend, in part, on where it stands on another issue: how it organizes the system of street justice. A system of street justice could be organized as a stand-alone reform. That is, peacemakers and elders could be recruited from the local community, trained, and employed to work among their peers. Alternatively, street justice could form part of a larger package of legal and social changes, such as Black's (1989: chap. 3) intriguing idea of legal cooperatives.

NOTES TO APPENDIX A

1. However, Maxfield treats the 15 percent of homicides classified as "other" as conflict homicides. Since 12 percent of these are committed between strangers and a further 16 percent between people of unknown relationship, this category is likely to contain some predatory homicides.

2. For purposes of this calculation, the following categories in Polk (1994: 23, table 1) were treated as nonmoralistic: "victims of parental suicide," "neonaticides," "homicides originating in other crimes," "victims of mass killers," "special cases," and "mercy killings." There are 102 cases of this kind, constituting 26.8 percent of the total number, or 28.5 percent of the total known cases.

# References

Abbott, Jack Henry. 1981. *In the belly of the beast: Letters from prison.* New York: Vintage Books.

Agnew, Robert. 1992. Foundation for a general strain theory of crime and delinquency. *Criminology* 30:47–87.

Akers, Ronald L. 1985. *Deviant behavior: A social learning approach.* 3d ed. Belmont, Calif.: Wadsworth.

Albrecht, Stan L., and Miles Green. 1977. Attitudes toward the police and the larger attitude complex: Implications for police-community relationships. *Criminology* 15:67–86.

Amis, Martin. 1989. *London fields.* New York: Harmony Books.

Anderson, Elijah. 1990. *Streetwise: Race, class, and change in an urban community.* Chicago: University of Chicago Press.

———. 1994. The code of the streets. *Atlantic Monthly* 273 (May): 81–94.

Anonymous. 1989. Homicide in the family. *Juristat Service Bulletin* 9:1.

Australian Bureau of Statistics. 1994. *Year Book Australia, 1994.* Canberra: Australian Bureau of Statistics.

———. 1996. *Year Book Australia, 1996.* Canberra: Australian Bureau of Statistics.

Ayers, Edward L. 1984. *Vengeance and justice: Crime and punishment in the 19th-century American South.* New York: Oxford University Press.

Bachman, Ronet. 1992. *Death and violence on the reservation: Homicide, family violence, and suicide in American Indian populations.* New York: Auburn House.

Baldus, David C., George Woodworth, and Charles A. Pulaski Jr. 1990. *Equal justice and the death penalty: A legal and empirical analysis.* Boston: Northeastern University Press.

Baldwin, James. 1966. A report from occupied territory. In *The price of the ticket: Collected nonfiction, 1948–1985,* 415–424. New York: St. Martin's Press, 1985.

Balikci, Asen. 1970. *The Netsilik Eskimos.* Garden City, N.Y.: Natural History Press.

Barth, Frederik. 1959. *Political leadership among Swat Pathans.* London: Athlone Press.

Barton, Roy Franklin. 1919. *Ifugao law.* Berkeley: University of California Press, 1969.

———. 1938. *Autobiographies of three pagans in the Philippines.* New Hyde Park, N.Y.: University Books, 1963.

Baumgartner, M. P. 1985. Law and the middle class: Evidence from a suburban town. *Law and Human Behavior* 9:3–24.

———. 1988. *The moral order of a suburb.* New York: Oxford University Press.

———. 1992. War and peace in early childhood. In *Virginia review of sociology,* vol. 1, *Law and conflict management,* edited by James Tucker, 1–38. Greenwich: JAI Press.

———. 1993. Violent networks: The origins and management of domestic conflict. In *Aggression and violence: Social interactionist perspectives,* edited by Richard B. Felson and James T. Tedeschi, 209–231. Washington, D.C.: American Psychological Association.

Beck, E. M. 1996. Review of Nisbett and Cohen's *Culture of honor: The psychology of violence in the South. Georgia Historical Quarterly* 80:922–924.

Beckerman, Stephen, and Roberto Lizarralde. 1995. State-tribal warfare and male-biased casualties among the Barí. *Current Anthropology* 36:497–506.

Bennett Ross, Jane. 1984. Effect of contact on revenge hostilities among the Achuarä Jívaro. In *Warfare, culture, and environment,* edited by R. Brian Ferguson, 83–109. Orlando: Academic Press.

Berger, Peter, Brigitte Berger, and Hansfried Kellner. 1973. *The homeless mind: Modernization and consciousness.* New York: Random House.

Bernard, Thomas J. 1990. Angry aggression among the "truly disadvantaged." *Criminology* 28:73–96.

Bing, Léon. 1991. *Do or die.* New York: HarperCollins.

Black, Donald. 1970. Production of crime rates. *American Sociological Review* 35:733–748.

———. 1971. The social organization of arrest. *Stanford Law Review* 23:1087–1111.

———. 1976. *The behavior of law.* New York: Academic Press.

———. 1980. *The manners and customs of the police.* New York: Academic Press.

———. 1983. Crime as social control. *American Sociological Review* 48:34–45.

———. 1987. Compensation and the social structure of misfortune. *Law and Society Review* 21:563–584.

———. 1989. *Sociological justice.* New York: Oxford University Press.

———. 1993a. The elementary forms of conflict management. In *The social structure of right and wrong,* chap. 5. San Diego: Academic Press, 1993.

———. 1993b. *The social structure of right and wrong.* San Diego: Academic Press.

———. 1994. Criminology as a subculture. Presentation at author-meets-critics session on *The social structure of right and wrong,* annual meeting of the American Society of Criminology, Miami.

———. 1995. The epistemology of pure sociology. *Law and Social Inquiry* 20:829–870.

——— 1998. Prologue to *The social structure of right and wrong.* 2d ed. San Diego: Academic Press. Forthcoming.

Black, Donald, and M. P. Baumgartner. 1980. On self-help in modern society. In *The manners and customs of the police,* by Donald Black, 193–208. New York: Academic Press.

———. 1983. Toward a theory of the third party. In *Empirical theories about courts,* edited by Keith O. Boyum and Lynn Mather, 84–114. New York: Longman.

Black-Michaud, Jacob. 1975. *Cohesive force: Feud in the Mediterranean and the Middle East.* Oxford: Basil Blackwell.

Blau, Judith R., and Peter M. Blau. 1982. The cost of inequality: Metropolitan structure and violent crime. *American Sociological Review* 47:114–129.

Blee, Katherine M., and Dwight B. Billings. 1996. Violence and local state formation: A longitudinal study of Appalachian feuding. *Law and Society Review* 30:671–705.

Block, Carolyn Rebecca. 1986. *Homicide in Chicago: Aggregate and time series perspectives on victim, offender and circumstances (1965–1981).* Chicago: Center for Urban Policy, Loyola University of Chicago.

Block, Carolyn Rebecca, and Antigone Christakos. 1995. Chicago homicide from the sixties to the nineties: Major trends in lethal violence. In

*Trends, risks, and interventions in lethal violence: Proceedings of the Third Annual Spring Symposium of the Homicide Research Working Group,* edited by Carolyn Block and Richard Block, 17–50. Washington, D.C.: National Institute of Justice.

Block, Richard. 1977. *Violent crime: Environment, interaction, and death.* Lexington, Mass.: Lexington-Heath.

Bodley, John H. 1990. *Victims of progress.* 3d ed. Mountain View, Calif.: Mayfield.

Boehm, Christopher. 1984. *Blood revenge: The enactment and management of conflict in Montenegro and other tribal societies.* Philadelphia: University of Pennsylvania Press.

Bohannan, Paul, ed. 1960a. *African homicide and suicide.* New York: Atheneum, 1967.

———. 1960b. Patterns of murder and suicide. In *African homicide and suicide,* 230–266. New York: Atheneum, 1967.

Borg, Marian. 1992. Conflict management in the modern world-system. *Sociological Forum* 7:261–282.

Boswell, Terry, and William J. Dixon. 1990. Dependency and rebellion: A cross-national analysis. *American Sociological Review* 55:540–559.

Bourdieu, Pierre. 1966. The sentiment of honour in Kabyle society. In *Honour and shame: The values of Mediterranean society,* edited by J. G. Peristiany, 191–241. Chicago: University of Chicago Press.

Bourgois, Philippe. 1995. *In search of respect: Selling crack in el Barrio.* New York: Cambridge University Press.

Braithwaite, John, and Philip Pettit. 1994. Republican criminology and victim advocacy. *Law and Society Review* 28:765–776.

Brearly, H. C. 1932. *Homicide in the United States.* Chapel Hill: University of North Carolina Press.

Brownfield, David. 1986. Social class and violent behavior. *Criminology* 24:421–438.

Brundage, W. Fitzhugh. 1993. *Lynching in the new South: Georgia and Virginia, 1880–1930.* Urbana: University of Illinois Press.

Bureau of the Census. 1996. *Statistical abstract of the United States, 1996.* Washington, D.C.: United States Department of Commerce.

Bursik, Robert J., and Harold G. Grasmick. 1993. *Neighborhoods and crime: The dimensions of effective community control.* New York: Lexington Books.

Butterfield, Fox. 1995. *All God's children: The Bosket family and the American tradition of violence.* New York: Avon Books.

Canada, Geoffrey. 1995. *Fist stick knife gun: A personal history of violence in America.* Boston: Beacon Press.

Cannavale, Frank J., Jr., and William D. Falcon. 1976. *Witness cooperation: With a handbook of witness management.* Lexington, Mass.: D. C. Heath.

Caplan, G. 1976. Studying the police. Address, Executive Forum on Upgrading the Police, Washington, D.C., April 13.

Carneiro, Robert L. 1970. A theory of the origin of the state. *Science* 169:733–738.

Carter, David L. 1983. Hispanic interaction with the criminal justice system in Texas: Experiences, attitudes, and perceptions. *Journal of Criminal Justice* 11:213–227.

Chagnon, Napoleon. 1977. *Yanomamö: The fierce people.* 2d ed. New York: Holt, Rinehart, and Winston.

———. 1988. Life histories, blood revenge, and warfare in a tribal population. *Science* 239:985–992.

Christie, Nils. 1977. Conflicts as property. *British Journal of Criminology* 17:1–15.

Colson, Elizabeth. 1953. Social control and vengeance in Plateau Tonga society. *Africa* 23:199–212.

———. 1974. *Tradition and contract: The problem of order.* Chicago: Aldine.

Cooney, Mark. 1986. Behavioral sociology of law: A defence. *Modern Law Review* 49:262–271.

———. 1988. The social control of homicide: A cross-cultural study. S.J.D. diss., Harvard Law School.

———. 1991. Law, morality, and conscience: The social control of homicide in modern America. Ph.D. diss., University of Virginia.

———. 1994. Evidence as partisanship. *Law and Society Review* 28:833–858.

———. 1997a. From warre to tyranny: Lethal conflict and the state. *American Sociological Review* 62:316–338.

———. 1997b. The decline of elite homicide. *Criminology* 35:381–407.

———. 1998. The dark side of community: Moralistic homicide and strong social ties. *Sociological Focus,* forthcoming.

Courtwright, David T. 1996. *Violent land: Single men and social disorder from the frontier to the inner city.* Cambridge: Harvard University Press.

Cragg, Wesley. 1992. *The practice of punishment: Towards a theory of restorative punishment.* London: Routledge.

Daly, Martin, and Margo Wilson. 1982. Homicide and kinship. *American Anthropologist* 84:372–378.

———. 1988. *Homicide*. Hawthorne, N.Y.: Aldine De Gruyter.

Danzig, Richard. 1973. Toward the creation of a complementary, decentralized system of criminal justice. *Stanford Law Review* 26:1–54.

Davis, Robert C., Victor Russell, and Victor Kunreuther. 1980. *The role of the complaining witness in an urban criminal court*. New York: Vera Institute of Justice and Victim Services Agency.

Dawson, John M., and Barbara Boland. 1993. *Murder in large urban counties, 1988*. Washington, D.C.: U.S. Department of Justice.

Decker, Scott. 1993. Exploring victim-offender relationships in homicide: The role of individual and event characteristics. *Justice Quarterly* 10:587–612.

Decker, Scott H., and Barrik Van Winkle. 1996. *Life in the gang: Family, friends, and violence*. Cambridge: Cambridge University Press.

Dentan, Robert K. 1978. Notes on childhood in a nonviolent context: The Semai case. In *Learning non-aggression: The experience of non-literate societies,* edited by Ashley Montagu, 94–143. New York: Oxford University Press.

———. 1979. *The Semai: A non-violent people of Malaya*. Fieldwork ed. New York: Holt, Rinehart and Winston.

———. 1988. Comment on "Reconsidering violence in simple human societies," by Bruce M. Knauft. *Current Anthropology* 29:625–629.

Dietz, Mary Lorenz. 1983. *Killing for profit: The social organization of felony homicide*. Chicago: Nelson-Hall.

Donaldson, Greg. 1993. *The Ville: Cops and kids in urban America*. New York: Ticknor and Fields.

Donne, John. [1624] 1959. *Devotions upon emergent occasions and several steps in my sickness*. Ann Arbor: University of Michigan Press.

Donziger, Steven R., ed. 1996. *The real war on crime: The report of the National Criminal Justice Commission*. New York: Harper.

Draper, Patricia. 1978. The learning environment for aggression and antisocial behavior among the !Kung. In *Learning non-aggression: The experience of non-literate societies,* edited by Ashley Montagu, 31–53. New York: Oxford University Press.

Durham, Mary E. 1909. *High Albania*. London: Edward Arnold.

Durkheim, Emile. [1893] 1964. *The Division of Labor in Society*. New York: Free Press.

———. [1899–1900] 1969. Two laws of penal evolution. *University of Cincinnati Law Review* 38:32–60.

Ekland-Olson, Sheldon. 1986. Crowding, social control, and prison violence: Evidence from the post-*Ruiz* years in Texas." *Law and Society Review* 20:389–421.

Elias, Norbert. [1939] 1978. *The civilizing process,* vol. 1, *The development of manners.* New York: Urizen Books.

———. [1939] 1982. *The civilizing process,* vol. 2, *Power and civility.* New York: Pantheon.

———. 1987. The retreat of sociologists into the present. *Theory, Culture and Society* 4:223–247.

Ellickson, Robert C. 1991. *Order without law: How neighbors settle disputes.* Cambridge: Harvard University Press.

Elwin, Verrier. 1950. *Maria murder and suicide.* 2d ed. Bombay: Oxford University Press.

Ember, Carol R., and Melvin Ember. 1994. War, socialization, and interpersonal violence. *Journal of Conflict Resolution* 38:620–646.

Ember, Carol R., Melvin Ember, and Bruce Russett. 1992. Peace between participatory polities: A cross-cultural test of the "democracies rarely fight each other" hypothesis. *World Politics* 44:573–599.

Ember, Carol R., Marc Howard Ross, Michael L. Burton, and Candace Bradley. 1991. Problems of measurement in cross-cultural research using secondary data. *Behavior Science Research* 25:187–216.

Ericksen, Karen Paige, and Heather Horton. 1992. "Blood feuds": Cross-cultural variations in kin group vengeance. *Behavior Science Research* 26:57–85.

Evans-Pritchard, E. E. 1940. *The Nuer: A description of the modes of livelihood and political institutions of a Nilotic people.* London: Oxford University Press.

Federal Bureau of Investigation. 1996. *Crime in the United States: Uniform Crime Reports, 1995.* Washington, D.C.: U.S. Department of Justice.

Feeley, Malcolm M. 1979. *The process is the punishment: Handling cases in a lower criminal court.* New York: Russell Sage Foundation.

Felson, Richard B. 1978. Aggression as impression management. *Social Psychology* 41:205–213.

———. 1982. Impression management and the escalation of aggression and violence. *Social Psychology Quarterly* 45:245–254.

―――. 1983. Aggression and violence between siblings. *Social Psychology Quarterly* 46:271–285.

―――. 1984. Patterns of aggressive social interaction. In *Social psychology of aggression: From individual behavior to social interaction,* edited by Amelie Mummedey, 107–126. Berlin: Springer-Verlag.

Felson, Richard B., Stephen A. Ribner, and Merryl S. Siegel. 1984. Age and the effect of third parties during criminal violence. *Sociology and Social Research* 68:452–462.

Felson, Richard B., and Natalie Russo. 1988. Parental punishment and sibling aggression. *Social Psychology Quarterly* 51:11–18.

Felson, Richard B., and Henry J. Steadman. 1983. Situational factors in disputes leading to criminal violence. *Criminology* 21:59–74.

Felson, Richard B., and James T. Tedeschi. 1993. A social interactionist approach to violence: Cross-cultural applications. *Violence and Victims* 8:295–310.

Ferguson, R. Brian. 1995. *Yanomami warfare: A political history.* Santa Fe: School of American Research Press.

Ferguson, R. Brian, and Neil L. Whitehead, eds. 1992. *War in the tribal zone: Expanding states and indigenous warfare.* Santa Fe: School of American Research Press.

Fox, Robin. 1962. Myths and fighting. In *Encounter with anthropology,* 153–175. New York: Harcourt Brace Jovanovich, 1968.

Freedman, Maurice. 1958. *Lineage organization in southeastern China.* London: Athlone Press.

Fried, Morton H. 1967. *The evolution of political society: An essay in political anthropology.* New York: Random House.

Friedrich, Paul. 1962. Assumptions underlying Tarascan political homicide. *Psychiatry* 25:315–327.

Fürer-Haimendorf, Christoph von. 1967. *Morals and merit: A study of values and social controls in South Asian societies.* Chicago: University of Chicago Press.

Gelles, Richard J. 1987. *The violent home.* Newbury Park, Calif.: Sage.

Gelles, Richard J., and Murray A. Strauss. 1988. *Intimate violence.* New York: Simon and Schuster.

Gibson, James L., and Gregory A. Caldeira. 1996. The legal cultures of Europe. *Law and Society Review* 30:55–85.

Gilsenan, Michael. 1976. Lying, honor, and contradiction. In *Transaction and meaning: Directions in the anthropology of exchange and symbolic behavior*, edited by Bruce Kapferer, 191–219. Philadelphia: Institute for the Study of Human Issues.

Ginat, Joseph. 1987. *Blood disputes among Bedouin and rural Arabs: Revenge, mediation, outcasting, and family honor.* London: University of Pittsburgh Press.

Given, James B. 1977. *Society and homicide in thirteenth-century England.* Stanford: Stanford University Press.

Gluckman, Max. 1969. *Custom and conflict in Africa.* New York: Barnes and Noble. Originally published in 1956.

Goetting, Ann. 1995. *Homicide in families and other special populations.* New York: Springer.

Gottfredson, Michael R., and Travis Hirschi. 1990. *A general theory of crime.* Stanford: Stanford University Press.

Graham, Michael H. 1985. *Witness intimidation: The law's response.* Westport, Conn.: Quorum Books.

Green, Edward, and Russell P. Wakefield. 1979. Patterns of middle and upper class homicide. *Journal of Criminal Law and Criminology* 70:172–181.

Greenberg, James B. 1989. *Blood ties: Life and violence in rural Mexico.* Tucson: University of Arizona Press.

Greene, Jack R., and Stephen D. Mastrofski, eds. 1988. *Community policing: Rhetoric or reality?* New York: Praeger.

Grönfors, Martti. 1986. Social control and law in the Finnish Gypsy community: Blood feuding as a system of justice. *Journal of Legal Pluralism* 24:101–125.

Gurr, Ted Robert. 1981. Historical trends in violent crime: A critical review of the evidence. In *Crime and justice: An annual review of research,* vol. 3, edited by Michael Tonry and Norval Morris, 295–353. Chicago: University of Chicago Press.

Hagedorn, John M. 1988. *People and folks: Gangs, crime and the underclass in a rustbelt city.* Chicago: Lake View Press.

Hallpike, C. R. 1977. *Bloodshed and vengeance in the Papuan Mountains: The generation of conflict in Tauade society.* Oxford: Clarendon Press.

Hanawalt, Barbara A. 1979. *Crime and conflict in English communities, 1300–1348.* Cambridge: Harvard University Press.

Harner, Michael J. 1972. *The Jívaro: People of the sacred waterfalls.* Garden City, N.Y.: Anchor Books.

Harrington, Christine B. 1984. The politics of participation and nonparticipation in dispute processes. *Law and Policy* 6:203–223.

―――. 1985. *Shadow justice: The ideology and institutionalization of alternatives to court.* Westport, Conn.: Greenwood Press.

Harrington, Christine B., and Sally Merry. 1988. The ideology of community mediation. *Law and Society Review* 22:709–735.

Hart, C. W. M., and Arnold R. Pilling. 1979. *The Tiwi of North Australia.* New York: Holt, Rinehart and Winston.

Hasluck, Margaret. 1954. *The unwritten law in Albania.* Cambridge: Cambridge University Press.

Hawkins, Darnell, ed. 1986. *Homicide among black Americans.* Lanham, Md.: University Press of America.

Heider, Karl. 1991. *Grand Valley Dani: Peaceful warriors.* 2d ed. New York: Holt, Rinehart and Winston.

Henry, Andrew F., and James F. Short Jr. 1954. *Suicide and homicide: Some economic, sociological, and psychological aspects of aggression.* New York: Free Press.

Hepburn, John R. 1973. Violent behavior in interpersonal relationships. *Sociological Quarterly* 14:419–429.

Hirschi, Travis. 1969. *Causes of delinquency.* Berkeley: University of California Press.

Hobbes, Thomas. [1651] 1909. *Leviathan.* Oxford: Clarendon Press.

Hoebel, E. Adamson. 1971. Feud: Concept, reality and method in the study of primitive law. In *Essays on modernization of underdeveloped societies,* vol. 1, edited by A. R. Desai, 500–513. Bombay: Thacker.

Hofer, Hans Von. 1990. Homicide in Swedish statistics, 1750–1988. In *Scandinavian studies in criminology,* vol. 11, edited by Annika Snare, 29–45. Oslo: Norwegian University Press.

Horowitz, Ruth. 1983. *Honor and the American dream: Culture and identity in a Chicano community.* New Brunswick: Rutgers University Press.

Horwitz, Allan V. 1982. *The social control of mental illness.* New York: Academic Press.

―――. 1983. Resistance to innovation in the sociology of law: A response to Greenberg. *Law and Society Review* 17:369–384.

―――. 1990. *The logic of social control.* New York: Plenum.

Howell, Signe and Roy Willis, eds. 1989. *Societies at peace: Anthropological perspectives.* London: Routledge.

Human Relations Area Files. 1967. The HRAF Quality Control Sample universe. *Behavior Science Notes* 2:81–88.

International Labor Office. 1992. *Yearbook of labor statistics.* Geneva: International Labor Office.

Irwin, John. 1980. *Prisons in turmoil.* Boston: Little, Brown.

Jacobs, James B. 1977. *Stateville: The penitentiary in mass society.* Chicago: University of Chicago Press.

James, Oliver. 1995. *Juvenile violence in a winner-loser culture: Socio-economic and familial origins of the rise of violence against the person.* London: Free Association Books.

Just, Peter. 1991. Going through the emotions: Passion, violence, and "other control" among the Dou Donggo. *Ethos* 19:288–312.

Kang, Gay Elizabeth. 1976. Conflicting loyalties theory: A cross-cultural test. *Ethnology* 15:201–210.

Katz, Jack. 1988. *Seductions of crime: Moral and sensual attractions in doing evil.* New York: Basic Books.

Keiser, R. Lincoln. 1986. Death enmity in Thull: Organized vengeance and social change in a Kohistani community. *American Ethnologist* 13:489–505.

Kelly, James. 1995. *'That damn'd thing called honour': Duelling in Ireland, 1570–1860.* Cork: Cork University Press.

Kessing, Roger M. 1975. *Kin groups and social structure.* New York: Holt, Rinehart and Winston.

Kiefer, Thomas M. 1972. *The Tausug: Violence and law in a Philippine Moslem society.* New York: Holt, Rinehart and Winston.

Kiernan, V. G. 1988. *The duel in European history: Honor and the reign of aristocracy.* Oxford: Oxford University Press.

Kinkead, Gwen. 1992. *Chinatown: A portrait of a closed society.* New York: HarperCollins.

Kleck, Gary. 1991. *Point blank: Guns and violence in America.* New York: Aldine De Gruyter.

Kleck, Gary, and David J. Bordua. 1983. The factual foundations for certain key assumptions of gun control. *Law and Policy Quarterly* 5:271–298.

Klein, Malcolm. 1971. *Street gangs and street workers.* Englewood Cliffs, N.J.: Prentice-Hall.

———. 1995. *The American street gang.* New York: Oxford University Press.

Klein, Malcolm W., and Cheryl L. Maxson. 1989. Street gang violence. In *Violent crime, violent criminals,* edited by Neil Alan Weiner and Marvin E. Wolfgang, 198–234. Newbury Park, Calif.: Sage.

Knauft, Bruce. 1985. *Good company and violence: Sorcery and social action in a lowland New Guinea society.* Berkeley: University of California Press.

———. 1987. Reconsidering violence in simple human societies. *Current Anthropology* 28:457–482.

———. 1990. Melanesian warfare: A theoretical history. *Oceania* 60:250–311.

Koch, Klaus-Friedrich. 1974. *War and peace in Jalémó: The management of conflict in highland New Guinea.* Cambridge: Cambridge University Press.

Koch, Klaus-Friedrich, and John A. Sodergen (with the collaboration of Susan Campbell). 1976. Political and psychological correlates of conflict management: A cross-cultural study. *Law and Society Review* 10:443–466.

Kposowa, Augustine J., and Kevin D. Breault. 1993. Reassessing the structural covariates of U.S. homicide rates: A county level study. *Sociological Focus* 26:27–46.

Kposowa, Augustine J., Gopal K. Singh, and K. D. Breault. 1994. The effect of marital status and social isolation on adult male homicides in the United States: Evidence from the National Longitudinal Mortality Study. *Journal of Quantitative Criminology* 10:277–289.

Kroeber, Theodora. 1961. *Ishi in two worlds: A biography of the last wild Indian in North America.* Berkeley: University of California Press.

Krohn, Marvin D. 1986. The web of conformity: A network approach to the explanation of deviant behavior. *Social Problems* 33:581–593.

———. 1995. Control and deterrence theories of criminality. In *Criminology: A Contemporary Handbook,* edited by Joseph F. Sheley, 329–347. Belmont, Calif.: Wadsworth.

Kropotkin, Peter. [1886] 1975. Law and authority. In *The essential Kropotkin,* edited by Emile Capouya and Keitha Tompkins, 27–43. New York: Liveright.

Land, Kenneth C., Patricia McCall, and Lawrence E. Cohen. 1990. Structural covariates of homicide rates: Are there any invariances across time and social space? *American Journal of Sociology* 95:922–963.

Landau, Simha F., and Israel Drapkin. 1968. *Ethnic patterns of criminal homicide in Israel.* Jerusalem: Institute of Criminology, Hebrew University.

Lane, Roger. 1997. *Murder in America: A history.* Columbus: Ohio State Press.

Launay, Gilles, and Peter Murray. 1989. Victim/offender groups. In *Medi-*

*ation and criminal justice: Victims, offenders and community,* edited by Martin Wright and Burt Galloway, 113–131. London: Sage.

Lee, Richard B. 1979. *The !Kung San: Men, women, and work in a foraging society.* Cambridge: Cambridge University Press.

———. 1993. *The Dobe Jul'hoansi.* 2d ed. Fort Worth: Harcourt Brace College Publishers.

Levi, Ken. 1980. Homicide as conflict resolution. *Deviant Behavior* 1:281–307.

Lewis, I. M. 1961. *A pastoral democracy: A study of pastoralism and politics among the northern Somali of the Horn of Africa.* London: Oxford University Press.

Lifton, Robert Jay. 1986. *The Nazi doctors: Medical killing and the psychology of genocide.* New York: Basic Books.

Lindholm, Charles. 1982. *Generosity and jealousy: The Swat Pukhtun of northern Pakistan.* New York: Columbia University Press.

Llewellyn, Karl N., and E. Adamson Hoebel. 1941. *The Cheyenne way: Conflict and case law in primitive jurisprudence.* Norman: University of Oklahoma Press.

Lowie, Robert H. 1954. *Indians of the Plains.* New York: McGraw-Hill.

Luckenbill, David F. 1977. Criminal homicide as a situated transaction. *Social Problems* 25:176–186.

Lundsgaarde, Henry P. 1977. *Murder in space city: A cultural analysis of Houston homicide patterns.* New York: Oxford University Press.

Lynch, Michael J., and W. Byron Groves. 1989. *A primer in radical criminology.* 2d ed. New York: Harrow and Heston.

MacKellar, F. Landis, and Machiko Yanagishita. 1995. *Homicide in the United States: Who's at risk?* Washington, D.C.: Population Reference Bureau.

Maguire, Kathleen, Ann L. Pastore, and Timothy J. Flanagan, eds. 1993. *Sourcebook of criminal justice statistics, 1992.* Washington, D.C.: U.S. Department of Justice.

Majors, Richard, and Janet Mancini Billson. 1992. *Cool pose: The dilemmas of black manhood in America.* New York: Lexington Books.

Mann, Coramae Richey. 1996. *When women kill.* Albany: State University of New York Press.

Manning, Peter K. 1977. *Police work: The social organization of policing.* Cambridge: MIT Press.

Marshall, Joseph, Jr., and Lonnie Wheeler. 1996. *Street soldier: One man's struggle to save a generation—One life at a time.* New York: Delacorte Press.

Martinez, Ramiro, Jr. 1996. Latinos and lethal violence: the impact of poverty and inequality. *Social Problems* 43:131–145.

Masumura, Wilfred T. 1977. Law and violence: A cross-cultural study. *Journal of Anthropological Research* 33:388–399.

Maxfield, Michael G. 1989. Circumstances in supplementary homicide reports: Variety and validity. *Criminology* 27:671–695.

Maxson, Cheryl L., and Malcolm W. Klein. 1990. Street gang violence: Twice as great, or half as great? In *Gangs in America,* edited by C. Ronald Huff, 71–100. Newbury Park, Calif.: Sage.

McBarnet, Doreen. 1981. *Conviction: Law, the state and the construction of justice.* London: Macmillan.

McCall, Nathan. 1994. *Makes me wanna holler: A young black man in America.* New York: Vintage.

McGrath, Roger D. 1984. *Gunfighters, highwaymen, and vigilantes: Violence on the frontier.* Berkeley: University of California Press.

———. 1989. Violence and lawlessness of the Western frontier. In *Violence in America,* vol. 1, *The history of crime,* edited by Ted Robert Gurr, 122–145. Newbury Park. Calif.: Sage.

McNight, David. 1986. Fighting in an Australian Aboriginal supercamp. In *The anthropology of violence,* edited by David McNight, 136–163. Oxford: Basil Blackwell.

Meares, Tracey, and Dan M. Kahan. 1997. Law and (norms of) order in the inner-city. Paper presented at the annual meeting of the Law and Society Association, St. Louis, Missouri.

Meggitt, Mervyn. 1977. *Blood is their argument: Warfare among the Mae Enga tribesmen of the New Guinea highlands.* Palo Alto: Mayfield.

Merry, Sally Engle, and Neal Milner, eds. 1993. *The possibility of popular justice: A case study of community mediation in the United States.* Ann Arbor: University of Michigan Press.

Merry, Sally Engle, and Susan Silbey. 1984. What do plaintiffs want? Reexamining the concept of dispute. *Justice System Journal* 9:151–178.

Merton, Robert K. 1940. Social structure and anomie. *American Sociological Review* 3:672–682.

———. 1968. The Matthew effect in science. *Science* 159:55–63.

Messmer, Heinz, and Hans-Uwe Otto, eds. 1992. *Restorative justice on trial: Pitfalls and potentials of victim-offender mediation—international research perspectives.* Dordrecht: Kluwer Academic Publishers.

Messner, Steven F. 1983. Regional and racial effects on the urban homicide rate: The subculture of violence revisited. *American Journal of Sociology* 88:997–1007.

Messner, Steven F., and Richard Rosenfeld. 1994. *Crime and the American dream.* Belmont, Calif.: Wadsworth.

Middleton, John. 1965. *The Lugbara of Uganda.* New York: Holt, Rinehart and Winston.

Miller, Walter B. 1958. Lower class culture as a generating milieu of gang delinquency. *Journal of Social Issues* 14:5–19.

Miller, William Ian. 1990. *Bloodtaking and peacemaking: Feud, law, and society in saga Iceland.* Chicago: University of Chicago Press.

Moore, Joan W., with Robert Garcia, Carole Garcia, Luis Cerda, and Frank Valencia. 1978. *Homeboys: Gangs, drugs, and prison in the barrios of Los Angeles.* Philadelphia: Temple University Press.

Moore, Sally Falk. 1972. Legal liability and evolutionary interpretation: Some aspects of strict liability, self-help, and collective responsibility. In *The allocation of responsibility,* edited by Max Gluckman, 51–107. Manchester: Manchester University Press.

Morrill, Calvin. 1995. *The executive way: Conflict management in corporations.* Chicago: University of Chicago Press.

Morrill, Calvin, and Cindy McKee. 1993. Institutional isomorphism and informal social control: Evidence from a community mediation center. *Social Problems* 40:445–463.

Muller, Edward N. 1985. Income inequality, regime repressiveness, and political violence. *American Sociological Review* 50:47–61.

Murphy, Robert F. 1957. Intergroup hostility and social cohesion. *American Anthropologist* 59:1018–1035.

Nader, Laura. 1990. *Harmony ideology: Justice and control in a Zapotec mountain village.* Stanford: Stanford University Press.

Næshagen, Ferdinand Linthoe. 1995. The drastic decline of Norwegian homicide rates between 1550 and 1800. Paper presented at the annual meeting of the American Society of Criminology, Boston.

Naroll, Raoul. 1967. The proposed HRAF probability sample. *Behavior Science Notes* 2:70–80.

Nash, June. 1967. Death as a way of life: The increasing resort to homicide in a Maya Indian community. *American Anthropologist* 69:445–470.

Nettler, Gwynn. 1982. *Killing one another.* Cincinnati: Anderson.

Ngor, Haing. 1987. *A Cambodian Odyssey.* New York: Macmillan.

Nisbett, Richard E., and Dov Cohen. 1996. *Culture of honor: The psychology of violence in the south.* Boulder: Westview Press.

Nove, Alec. 1993. Victims of Stalinism: How many? In *Stalinist terror: New perspectives,* edited by J. Arch Getty and Roberta T. Manning, 261–274. Cambridge: Cambridge University Press.

———. 1994. Terror victims—is the evidence complete? *Europe-Asia Studies* 46:535–537.

Oliver, William. 1994. *The violent social world of black men.* New York: Lexington Books.

Österberg, Eva. 1996. Criminality, social control, and the early modern state: Evidence and interpretations in Scandanavian historiography. In *The civilization of crime: Violence in town and country since the middle ages,* edited by Eric A. Johnson and Eric H. Monkkonen, 35–62. Urbana: University of Illinois Press.

Otterbein, Keith F. 1968. Internal war: A cross-cultural study. *American Anthropologist* 70:277–289.

———. 1986. *The ultimate coercive sanction: A cross-cultural study of capital punishment.* New Haven: HRAF Press.

Otterbein, Keith F., and Charlotte Swanson Otterbein. 1965. An eye for an eye, a tooth for a tooth: A cross-cultural study of feuding. *American Anthropologist* 67:1470–1482.

Parker, Karen F., and Patricia L. McCall. 1997. Adding another piece to the inequality-homicide puzzle. *Homicide Studies* 1:35–60.

Paternoster, Raymond. 1991. *Capital punishment in America.* New York: Lexington Books.

Pearson, Jessica, and Nancy Thoennes. 1985. Mediation versus the courts in child custody cases. *Negotiation Journal* July: 235–245.

Pepinsky, Harold E., and Richard T. Quinney, eds. 1991. *Criminology as peacemaking.* Bloomington: Indiana University Press.

Peters, E. L. 1967. Some structural aspects of the feud among the camel-herding Bedouin of Cyrenaica. *Africa* 37:261–282.

———. 1975. Foreword to *Cohesive force: Feud in the Mediterranean and the Middle East,* by Jacob Black-Michaud, ix–xxvii. New York: St. Martin's Press.

Peterson, Ruth D., and Lauren J. Krivo. 1993. Racial segregation and black urban homicide. *Social Forces* 71:1001–1026.

Pilling, Arnold R. 1968. Remarks on "Predation and warfare." In *Man the hunter,* edited by Richard B. Lee and Irven DeVore, 158. Chicago: Aldine.

Pitt-Rivers, Julian. 1966. Honour and social status. In *Honour and shame: The values of Mediterranean society,* edited by J. G. Peristiany, 19–77. Chicago: University of Chicago Press.

Polk, Kenneth. 1994. *When men kill: Scenarios of masculine violence.* Cambridge: Cambridge University Press.

Porter, Bruce. 1982. California prison gangs: The price of control. *Corrections Magazine* 6 (December): 6–19.

Reiss, Albert J., Jr., and Jeffrey A. Roth, eds. 1993. *Understanding and preventing violence.* Washington, D.C.: National Academy Press.

Robarchek, Clayton A. 1977. Frustration, aggression, and the nonviolent Semai. *American Ethnologist* 4:762–769.

Robarchek, Clayton A., and Robert K. Dentan. 1987. Blood drunkenness and the bloodthirsty Semai. *American Anthropologist* 89:356–365.

Robarchek, Clayton A., and Carole J. Robarchek. 1992. Cultures of war and peace: A comparative study of Waorani and Semai. In *Aggression and peacefulness in human and other primates,* 189–213. New York: Oxford University Press.

Rodman, Margaret, and Matthew Cooper, eds. 1979. *The pacification of Melanesia.* Ann Arbor: University of Michigan Press.

Romanucci-Ross, Lola. 1973. *Conflict, violence, and morality in a Mexican village.* Chicago: University of Chicago Press.

Rosaldo, Renato. 1980. *Ilongot headhunting, 1883–1974: A study in society and history.* Stanford: Stanford University Press.

Rosenfeld, Richard, and Steven F. Messner. 1991. The social sources of homicide in different types of societies. *Sociological Forum* 6:51–70.

Ross, Marc Howard. 1986. A cross-cultural theory of political conflict and violence. *Political Psychology* 7:427–469.

———. 1993. *The culture of conflict: Interpretations and interests in comparative perspective.* New Haven: Yale University Press.

Ruggiero, Guido. 1980. *Violence in early Renaissance Venice.* New Brunswick: Rutgers University Press.

Rummel, R. J. 1990. *Lethal politics: Soviet genocide and mass murder since 1917.* New Brunswick, N.J.: Transaction Books.

———. 1991. *China's bloody century: Genocide and mass murder since 1900.* New Brunswick, N.J.: Transaction Books.

———. 1992. *Democide: Nazi genocide and mass murder.* New Brunswick, N.J.: Transaction Books.

———. 1994. *Death by government.* New Brunswick, N.J.: Transaction Books.

———. 1995. Democracy, power, genocide, and mass murder. *Journal of Conflict Resolution* 39:3–26.

Runnymede Trust and Radical Statistics Race Group. 1980. *Britain's black population.* London: Heinemann Educational Books.

Sampson, Robert J., and W. Byron Groves. 1989. Community structure and crime: Testing social-disorganization theory. *American Journal of Sociology* 94:774–802.

Sanders, William B. 1994. *Gangbangs and drive-bys: Grounded culture and juvenile gang violence.* Hawthorne, N.Y.: Aldine De Gruyter.

Saran, A. B. 1974. *Murder and suicide among the Munda and Oraon.* Delhi: National Publishing House.

Schwartz, Lola Romanucci. 1972. Conflict without violence and violence without conflict. In *Collective violence,* edited by James F. Short Jr. and Marvin E. Wolfgang, 149–158. Chicago: Aldine.

Schwendinger, Herman, and Julia Schwendinger. 1970. Defenders of order or guardians of human rights? *Issues in Criminology* 7:71–81.

Senechal de la Roche, Roberta. 1990. *The sociogenesis of a race riot: Springfield, Illinois, in 1908.* Urbana: University of Illinois Press.

———. 1996. Collective violence as social control. *Sociological Forum* 11:97–128.

Shakur, Sanyika. 1993. *Monster: The autobiography of an L.A. gang member.* New York: Penguin.

Shaw, Clifford R., and Henry D. McKay. 1969. *Juvenile delinquency and urban areas: A study of rates of delinquency in relation to differential characteristics of local communities in American cities.* Revised ed. Chicago: University of Chicago Press.

Sheley, Joseph F., and James D. Wright. 1995. *In the line of fire: Youth, guns, and violence in urban America.* New York: Aldine De Gruyter.

Sherman, Lawrence W. 1992. *Policing domestic violence.* New York: Free Press.

Shihadeh, Edward S., and Nicole Flynn. 1996. Segregation and crime: The effect of black social isolation on black urban violence. *Social Forces* 74:1325–1352.

Silberman, Matthew. 1995. *A world of violence: Corrections in America.* Belmont, Calif.: Wadsworth.

Silverman, Robert, and Leslie Kennedy. 1993. *Deadly deeds: Murder in Canada.* Scarborough, Ont.: Nelson Canada.

Simon, David. 1991. *Homicide: A year on the killing streets.* New York: Fawcett Columbine.

Singer, J. David, and Melvin Small. 1972. *The wages of war, 1816–1965: A Statistical Handbook.* New York: Wiley and Sons.

Smith, J. David, and Jeremy Gray. 1985. *Police and people in London: The PSI Report.* Aldershot: Gower.

Sorenson, E. Richard. 1972. Socio-ecological change among the Fore of New Guinea. *Current Anthropology* 13:349–372.

Spierenburg, Pieter. 1996. Long-term trends in homicide: Theoretical reflections and Dutch evidence, fifteenth to twentieth centuries. In *The civilization of crime: Violence in town and country since the Middle Ages,* edited by Eric A. Johnson and Eric H. Monkkonen, 63–105. Urbana: University of Illinois Press.

Stack, Steven. 1996. The southern subculture of violence and homicide: An analysis of individual level data, 1990. Paper presented at the annual meeting of the American Society of Criminology, Chicago.

Statistics Canada. 1992. *Education in Canada: A statistical review for 1990–91.* Ottawa: Statistics Canada.

Stewart, Frank. 1994. *Honor.* Chicago: University of Chicago Press.

Stirling, Paul. 1965. *Turkish village.* New York: Wiley and Sons.

Stone, Lawrence. 1965. *The crisis of the aristocracy, 1558–1641.* Oxford: Clarendon Press.

———. 1983. Interpersonal violence in English society, 1300–1980. *Past and Present* 101:22–33.

Strang, Heather. 1993. *Homicides in Australia, 1991–92.* Canberra: Australian Institute of Criminology.

Sutherland, Edwin. 1947. *Principles of criminology.* 4th ed. Philadelphia: Lippincott.

Suttles, Gerald D. 1968. *The social order of the slum.* Chicago: University of Chicago Press.

Tedeschi, James T., and Richard B. Felson. 1994. *Violence, aggression, and coercive actions.* Washington, D.C.: American Psychological Association.

Thoden van Velzen, H. U. E., and W. van Wetering. 1960. Residence, power groups, and intra-societal aggression: An enquiry into the conditions leading to peacefulness within non-stratified societies. *International Archives of Ethnography* 49:169–200.

———. 1987. Comments on Bruce Knauft's "Reconsidering violence in simple human societies." *Current Anthropology* 28:487–488.

Thomas, Elizabeth Marshall. 1994. Management of violence among the Ju/wasi of Nyae Nyae: The old way and the new way. In *Studying war: Anthropological perspectives,* edited by S. P. Reyna and R. E. Downs, 69–84. Langhorne, Pa.: Gordon and Breach.

Thrasher, Frederic M. 1927. *The gang: A study of 1,313 gangs in Chicago.* Chicago: University of Chicago Press.

Tilly, Charles. 1990. *Coercion, capital, and European states, A.D. 990–1992.* Cambridge: Blackwell.

Tittle, Charles R. 1983. Social class and criminal behavior: A critique of the theoretical foundation. *Social Forces* 62:334–358.

Tittle, Charles R., and Robert F. Meier. 1990. Specifying the SES/delinquency relationship. *Criminology* 28:271–299.

Tittle, Charles R., Wayne J. Villemez, and Douglas A. Smith. 1978. The myth of social class and criminality: An empirical assessment of the empirical evidence. *American Sociological Review* 43:643–656.

Tolnay, Stewart E., and E. M. Beck. 1995. *A festival of violence: An analysis of southern lynchings, 1882–1930.* Urbana: University of Illinois Press.

Tout, T. F. 1920. *Medieval forgerers and forgeries.* Manchester: Manchester University Press.

Toy, Calvin. 1992. A short history of Asian gangs in San Francisco. *Justice Quarterly* 9:647–665.

Trench, Charles Chenevix. 1984. *The great Dan: A biography of Daniel O'Connell.* London: Jonathan Cape.

Tucker, James. 1998. *The therapeutic corporation.* New York: Oxford University Press, forthcoming.

Tucker, James, and Susan Ross. 1998. A micro-structural theory of corporal punishment. In *Corporal punishment by parents in theoretical perspective,* edited by Michael Donnelly and Murray A. Straus. New Haven: Yale University Press, forthcoming.

Turnbull, Colin M. 1961. *The forest people.* New York: Simon and Schuster.

———. 1965. *Wayward servants: The two worlds of the African Pygmies.* Garden City, N.Y.: Natural History Press.

———. 1978. The politics of non-aggression. In *Learning non-aggression: The experience of non-literate societies,* edited by Ashley Montagu, 161–221. New York: Oxford University Press.

Umbreit, Mark. 1985. *Crime and reconciliation: Creative options for victims and offenders.* Nashville: Abingdon Press.

————. 1989. Violent offenders and their victims. In *Mediation and criminal justice: Victims, offenders and community,* edited by Martin Wright and Burt Galaway, 99–112. London: Sage.

United Nations. 1996. *Demographic yearbook, 1994.* New York: United Nations.

United States Department of Justice. 1994. *Partnerships against violence: Promising programs resource guide,* vol. 1. Washington, D.C.: U.S. Department of Justice.

Unnithan, N. Prabha, Lin Huff-Corzine, Jay Corzine, and Hugh P. Witt. 1994. *The currents of lethal violence: An integrated model of suicide and homicide.* Albany: State University of New York Press.

Vandal, Gilles. 1991. "Bloody Caddo": White violence against blacks in a Louisiana parish, 1865–1876. *Journal of Social History* 25:373–388.

van den Steenhoven, Geert. 1962. Leadership and law among the Eskimos of the Keewatin District, Northwest Territories. Ph.D. diss., University of Leiden.

Vigil, James Diego. 1988. *Barrio gangs: Street life and identity in southern California.* Austin: University of Texas Press.

Waegel, William B. 1981. Case routinization in investigative police work. *Social Problems* 28:263–275.

Waldron, Jarlath. 1992. *Maamtrasna: The murders and the mystery.* Dublin: Edmund Burke.

Wallace, Alison. 1986. *Homicide: The social reality.* Sydney: New South Wales Bureau of Crime Statistics and Research.

Wallace-Hadrill, J. M. 1959. The bloodfeud of the Franks. *Journal of the John Rylands Library* 41:459–487.

Waller, Altina L. 1988. *Feud: Hatfields, McCoys, and social change in Appalachia, 1860–1900.* Chapel Hill: University of North Carolina Press.

Warner, W. Lloyd. 1958. *A black civilization: A social study of an Australian tribe.* Revised ed. New York: Harper and Brothers.

Wheatcroft, Stephen G. 1992. More light on the scale of repression and excess mortality in the Soviet Union in the 1930s. *Soviet Studies* 42:355–367.

Wilbanks, William. 1984. *Murder in Miami: An analysis of homicide patterns and trends in Dade County (Miami), Florida, 1917–1983.* Lanham, Md.: University Press of America.

Williams, Jack K. 1980. *Dueling in the old South: Vignettes of social history.* College Station: Texas A&M University Press.

Williams, Kirk R., and Robert L. Flewelling. 1988. The social production of criminal homicide: A comparative study of disaggregated rates in American cities. *American Sociological Review* 53:421–431.

Wilson, Margo, and Martin Daly. 1993. An evolutionary psychology perspective on male sexual proprietariness and violence against wives. *Violence and Victims* 8:271–294.

Wittfogel, Karl A. 1957. *Oriental despotism: A comparative study of total power.* New Haven: Yale University Press.

Wolff, Edward N. 1995. *Top heavy: A study of the increasing inequality of wealth in America.* New York: Twentieth Century Fund Press.

Wolfgang, Marvin E. 1958. *Patterns in criminal homicide.* Philadelphia: University of Pennsylvania Press.

Wolfgang, Marvin E., and Franco Ferracuti. 1967. *The subculture of violence: Towards an integrated theory in criminology.* London: Tavistock.

Woodburn, James. 1979. Minimal politics: The political organization of the Hadza of North Tanzania. In *Politics in leadership,* edited by William A. Schak and Percy S. Cohen, 244–266. Oxford: Clarendon Press, 1979.

Wright, Christine. 1992. Homicide in Canada, 1991. *Juristat Service Bulletin* 12 (18).

Wright, Martin. 1982. *Making good: Prison, punishment and beyond.* London: Burnett Books.

Wright, Martin, and Burt Galaway, eds. 1989. *Mediation and criminal justice: Victims, offenders and community.* London: Sage.

Wyatt-Brown, Bertram. 1982. *Southern honor: Ethics and behavior in the old South.* New York: Oxford University Press.

Yost, James A. 1981. Twenty years of contact: The mechanisms of change in Wao ("Auca") culture. In *Cultural transformations and ethnicity in modern Ecuador,* edited by Norman E. Whitten Jr., 677–704. Urbana: University of Illinois Press.

Zahn, Margaret A., and Philip C. Sagi. 1987. Stranger homicides in nine American cities. *Journal of Criminal Law and Criminology* 78:377–397.

Zimmermann, H. G. 1966. Die Kriminalität der ausläandischern Arbeiter. *Kriminalistik* 2:623–625.

Zimring, Franklin E., Satyanshu K. Mukherjee, and Barrik Van Winkle. 1983. Intimate violence: A study of intersexual homicide in Chicago. *University of Chicago Law Review* 50:910–930.

# Author Index

198 | *Author Index*

Maxfield, Michael G., 155–156, 172n. 1, 186
Maxson, Cheryl L., 76, 183, 186
McBarnet, Doreen, 126, 186
McCall, Nathan, 118, 186
McCall, Patricia, 6, 16, 26, 28, 165n. 3, 166n. 4, 184, 188
McGrath, Roger D., 18, 109, 110, 128, 186
McKay, Henry D., 120, 152, 190
McKee, Cindy, 143, 187
McNight, David, 91, 186
Meares, Tracey, 149, 186
Meggitt, Mervyn, 80, 83, 186
Meier, Robert F., 30, 192
Merry, Sally Engle, 143, 149, 182, 186
Merton, Robert K., 135, 152, 186
Messmer, Heinz, 144, 187
Messner, Steven F., 51, 151, 152, 186, 189
Middleton, John, 52, 79, 98, 187
Miller, Walter B., 152, 187
Miller, William Ian, 3, 109, 187
Milner, Neal, 143, 186
Moore, Joan W., 18, 76, 187
Moore, Sally Falk, 167n. 3, 169n. 6, 187
Morrill, Calvin, 12, 139, 143, 187
Mukherjee, Satyanshu K., 137, 194
Muller, Edward N., 57, 186
Murphy, Robert F., 91, 188
Murray, Peter, 144, 184

Nader, Laura, 93–94, 187
Næshagen, Ferdinand Linthoe, 99, 187
Naroll, Raoul, 161, 187
Nash, June, 93, 187
Nettler, 28, 188
Ngor, Haing, 168n. 7, 188
Nisbett, Richard E., 121, 122, 170n. 2, 171n. 5, 188
Nove, Alec, 168n. 8, 188

Oliver, William, 17, 116, 188
Österberg, Eva, 99, 188

Otterbein, Charlotte Swanson, 51, 81, 188
Otterbein, Keith F., 51, 57, 81, 188
Otto, Hans-Uwe, 144, 187

Parker, Karen F., 166n. 4, 188
Pastore, Ann L., 125, 185
Paternoster, Raymond, 148, 188
Pearson, Jessica, 143, 188
Pepinsky, Harold E., 144, 189
Peters, E. L., 81, 98, 188
Peterson, Ruth D., 166n. 4, 188
Pettit, Philip, 144, 176
Pilling, Arnold R., 52, 89, 182, 188
Pitt-Rivers, Julian, 18, 109, 113, 122, 123, 189
Polk, Kenneth, 17, 24, 114, 117, 156, 172n. 2, 189
Porter, Bruce, 72, 189
Pulaski, Charles A., Jr., 9, 173

Quinney, Richard T., 144, 188

Reiss, Albert J., Jr., 28, 52, 77, 189
Ribner, Stephen A., 7, 180
*Richmond Times-Dispatch*, 86
Robarchek, Carole J., 49, 60, 62, 92–93, 189
Robarchek, Clayton A., 49, 60, 62, 92–93, 189
Rodman, Margaret, 52, 189
Romanucci-Ross, Lola, 93, 189
Rosaldo, Renato, 81, 157, 189
Rosenfeld, Richard, 51, 151, 152, 187, 189
Ross, Marc Howard, 51, 81, 91, 163, 179, 189
Ross, Susan, 103, 192
Roth, Jeffrey A., 28, 52, 77, 189
Ruggiero, Guido, 33, 189
Rummel, R. J., 56, 57, 58, 168n. 3, 189–190
Runnymede Trust and Radical Statistics Race Group, 124, 190
Russell, Victor, 123, 178
Russett, Bruce, 52, 179

# Subject Index

!Kung San. *See* Ju/'hoansi

Latinos, 28, 125, 139, 166–167n. 9
Law, 59, 63, 141, 148, 169n. 3, 171n.
   8; availability of, 11, 16, 31, 39–41,
   43, 65, 134–135; Black's theory of,
   8, 9–10, 40; and honor, 122–132,
   171n. 6; hostility to in United
   States, 86, 124–127, 149; hostility
   to in other societies, 127–129, 149;
   manipulation of, 129–132; and
   street justice, 147–148; and violence, 8, 11, 50, 62–66, 149, 171n.
   8. *See also* Courts; Judges; Lawyers;
   Legal officials; Prosecutors; State;
   Statelessness
Lawyers, 9, 39, 102, 123, 127. *See also*
   Legal officials
Lebanon, 111
Legal officials, 6, 7–8, 16, 23, 39–40,
   41, 43, 53, 55, 65, 86, 104, 122,
   123, 124–129, 147, 167n. 10, 170n.
   13, 171n. 6. *See also* Judges;
   Lawyers; Police; Prosecutors
Legal settlement. *See* Settlement, infor-
   mal and legal compared
Lermontov, Mikhail, Iurevich, 35
Lethal assault. *See* Homicide
Lethal conflict. *See* Homicide
Lethal vengeance. *See* Homicide;
   Vengeance
Lethal violence. *See* Homicide
Liability, collective, 75–76
London, 124, 157
Los Angeles, 18, 76, 79, 84, 95–96,
   124
Lugbara, 79, 98, 163
Lynching, 12, 36–37, 43

Mae Enga, 80, 82–83
Magistrate, 62
Malaya, 49, 63, 92
Manchu China, 163
Manslaughter, 4–5
Marginality. *See* Radial status
Maria Gond, 157, 162, 163

Marital status, 26–27, 39
Marriage. *See* Marital status
Mbuti Pygmies, 3
Mediation, 7, 59–60, 61, 65, 143, 144,
   146, 149
Mediators, 11, 38, 91
Medicine, 13, 50, 53, 168n. 7
Mexico, 24, 93, 164
Miami, 15
Milwaukee, 18
Minorities: and homicide, 2, 25–26,
   27–28, 56, 72; and law, 40,
   123–129, 145; and violence, 40,
   139, 145
Modernization, 94–95, 99–101
Montenegro, 81, 110, 112
Moralism, 11, 38–39, 104–105, 141
Moralistic violence. *See* Violence, as
   morality
Munda, 157
Murder. *See* Homicide
Murngin, 89, 164

Negotiation, 11, 39
Neighbors, 6, 59, 64, 68, 91, 101
New Guinea, 3, 18, 32, 53, 80, 82
New South Wales, 15, 25
New York, 18, 25, 68, 101, 116, 120,
   123, 124, 125, 126, 129, 145
Nigeria, 147
Nonlethal violence, 13, 85, 136, 137.
   *See also* Assault
Nonpartisanship, 68; cold, 70, 72, 96,
   99, 101, 103; and third party social
   ties, 89–106, 170n. 11; and vio-
   lence, 103–104; warm, 70, 72, 90
Nonviolence. *See* Peace
Normative status, 9, 24, 28–29, 39, 40,
   131, 146
North America, 16, 18, 49. *See also*
   Canada; United States
Northumberland, earl of, 101
Norway, 99
Nuer, 18, 91, 109, 110, 163

Oaxaca, 93

# About the Author

Mark Cooney holds a doctoral degree in law from Harvard Law School and in sociology from the University of Virginia. He is currently Assistant Professor of Sociology and Adjunct Assistant Professor of Law at the University of Georgia. A native of Ireland, he has previously been a member of faculty at University College Dublin and the University of Zimbabwe.